The Pocket Green Book

Andrew Rees

Zed Books Ltd
London and New Jersey

The Pocket Green Book: The Environmental Crisis in a Nutshell
was first published by Zed Books Ltd, 57 Caledonian Road,
London N1 9BU, United Kingdom
and 171 First Avenue, Atlantic Highlands, New Jersey 07716,
United States of America

Typeset by EMS Photosetters, Thorpe Bay, Essex
Cover design by The Third Man
Photo credit: European Space Agency/Science Photo Library
Printed and bound in the United Kingdom by
Cox and Wyman Ltd, Reading

British Library Cataloguing in Publication Data

Rees, Andrew
  The pocket green book.
  1. Environment. Conservation.
  I. Title.
  333.72

  ISBN 0-86232-998-1
  ISBN 0-86232-999-X pbk.

Library of Congress Cataloging-in-Publication Data

Rees, Andrew.
  The pocket green book : the environmental
  crisis in a nutshell/Andrew Rees.
     p.   cm.
  Includes bibliographical references (p. 130).
  ISBN 0-86232-998-1 (cloth)
  ISBN 0-86232-999-X (pbk.)
  1. Pollution – Popular works. 2. Human
  ecology – Popular works. I. Title.
  TD175.R44   1991
  363.7–dc20   90-27384
                      CIP

Contents

Acknowledgements

I make no claim that the ideas in this book are original; the presentation is, though, I believe. I would, therefore, like to thank all the authors whose material has been so vital in compiling this volume.

About the Book

Soaking in the bath one night, it came to me that there was no overview of the environmental crisis, no thorough but simple book, written for the general public. However, if we are to win the battle for the environment, it will only happen by people rising up around the world and demanding change. And this can only happen when people are informed about what is going on and what can be done about it. Hence, I have condensed this complex subject into a hundred or so short pages – compiled a sort of instant environmental 'knowledge kit'. In this way, and by donating half of my royalties, I hope to make a contribution to our beleaguered planet and the beauty of the natural world I love so passionately.

To this beautiful planet, an endangered species.

This Earth is Precious

In 1854 the 'Great White Chief' in Washington made an offer for a large area of Indian land and promised a 'reservation' for the Indian people. Below is part of Chief Seattle's reply.

. . . Every part of this earth is sacred to my people.

Every shining pine needle, every sandy shore, every mist in the dark woods, every clearing and humming insect is holy in the memory and experience of my people . . .

We know that the white man does not understand our ways . . .

The sight of your cities pains the eyes of the red man. But perhaps it is because the red man is a savage and does not understand.

There is no quiet place in white man's cities. No place to hear the unfurling of leaves in spring, or the rustle of an insect's wings.

But perhaps it is because I am a savage and do not understand.

The clatter only seems to insult the ears. And what is there to life if a man cannot hear the lonely cry of a whippoorwill or the arguments of the frogs around the pond at night? I am a red man and do not understand . . .

The white man does not seem to notice the air he breathes. Like a man dying for many days, he is numb to the stench . . .

I am a savage and I do not understand any other way.

I have seen a thousand rotting buffaloes on the prairie, left by the white man who shot them from a passing train.

I am a savage and I do not understand how the smoking iron horse can be more important than the buffalo that we kill only to stay alive.

What is man without the beasts? If all the beasts were gone, man would die from a great loneliness of spirit.

1

Introduction

THE STATE OF THE WORLD

The number one priority on the international agenda is now the environmental crisis. If we don't sort this out, civilization will collapse and life on earth as we know it – humankind included – will be obliterated.

1990 – and the pace of environmental deterioration continiues to accelerate, with truly terrifying consequences. Tropical rainforests are being annihilated so quickly they will be virtually gone by 2000.[1] The ozone layer, vital for survival, is thinning at frightening rates. Acid rain is destroying huge areas of forest and tens of thousands of lakes in the Northern Hemisphere. We treat rivers, lakes, and oceans like open sewers; and we pollute the sky as though we didn't have to breathe the air. Our numbers will increase at a terrifying average of 96 million each year during the 1990s, so there will be 6.25 billion of us by 2000[2] – outstripping food production at an alarming rate. Already, 20% of humanity are so poor they cannot earn the means to the most meagre existence.[3] We gobble resources as though they were inexhaustible or we had a couple of spare planets parked out in space. We destroy natural habitats in every corner of the globe with little concern for the consequences; turning enchanted landscapes into eyesores. We slaughter the world's most beautiful animals as though profits justify their extinction, and we drive thousands (soon millions) more species the same way as the tropical rainforests fall. Soil, the basis of civilization, is eroded so effectively that America has lost $\frac{1}{3}$ of her topsoil.[4] And deserts are expanding so rapidly they threaten to cover $\frac{1}{3}$ of the earth.[3] Worst of all, the earth is steadily warming with potentially devastating effects.

If we want the earth to remain habitable for our children, we have to introduce fundamental changes NOW.

REASONS FOR HOPE

Environmental destruction has never been greater, but there are reasons for hope. The last few years have seen a spate of international conferences and agreements. In October 1987, the UN-established Brundtland Report (chaired by Norway's then Prime Minister Gro Harlem Brundtland) called for a new focus on sustainable development. The 1987 Montreal Protocol, involving 24 nations, has restricted the use of CFCs, and is an encouraging example of international co-operation. In 1989, the World Bank tentatively elevated environmental concern to a more central position in its development policy; and the Group of Seven's annual summit meeting spent much of the weekend discussing the Greenhouse Effect (GE), deforestation, and ozone depletion. And the deepest split of all – between East and West – is being reduced.

Everywhere, politicians, the media, industrialists are saying (though not yet doing) things not even dreamt of as possible a few years ago. But most importantly, 1989 and 1990 saw an enormous mushrooming of public awareness and concern for the environment. Everywhere, green issues are in the media daily. Green Consumerism is becoming the rage. And in the June 1989 European elections, the Greens doubled their seats to 39 out of 518 (the leading Socialists got 180), with the French Greens getting 11% of the vote, and the British 15%, up from less than 1% in 1984! Nationally, the Greens hold nearly 6% of seats in Sweden, and a very impressive 14% in the Australian state of Tasmania. In France, they captured 1,800 city council seats in 1989. In the same year, Holland, Norway, and Australia announced long-term environmental plans of varying comprehensiveness; and a UN-commission poll in 14 politically varied countries found in every area of the world nothing less than alarm about the environment.[2] The Green Movement is gaining momentum, and the politicians know it. We could be on the brink of one of the biggest attitude changes in history.

2

2
The Greenhouse Effect

INTRODUCTION

The Greenhouse Effect (GE) is the artificial warming of the atmosphere by man-made pollutant gases. It is now the most serious environmental issue.

Carbon dioxide – the major Greenhouse gas – is vital in controlling global climate, and without it the earth would be too cold to be habitable. It lets through most of the sun's incoming energy (short wave), but absorbs much that bounces off the earth's surface out towards space (long wave). But as it and the other Greenhouse gases increase, the earth is getting too warm, with potentially catastrophic consequences.

NASA's Dr James Hansen said all this heat is no mere statistical fluke. 'It is time to stop waffling so much and say that the evidence is pretty strong that the greenhouse effect is here.'[1]

CAUSES

These are many and are best seen by studying the Greenhouse gases.

Carbon dioxide

At 7–8 billion tons globally per annum, this is society's largest waste product,[2] accounting for approximately 50% of the GE.[1] Atmospheric levels have risen 13% since mid-century, and are still increasing.[3]

Burning fossil fuels □ Burning coal, oil, natural gas for electricity generation, steel making, and car exhausts, produce 5.7 billion tons of this (the equivalent to 190 million fully loaded 30 ton trucks), and in 1988, rates were rising by 3.7%.[3] The US is responsible for a full 20% of this, the USSR the same.[2] At 5 tons per year, the US is the largest per capita producer of carbon dioxide (and also produces 20% of all Greenhouse emissions[4]);

the global average is just over 1 ton.[2] (See *The Transport Problem*; *Energy*.)

Tropical rainforest (TRF) destruction □ The massive felling and burning of the TRFs is the second largest source of carbon dioxide, accounting for 20–25% of emissions and 0.9–2.5 billion tons.[2] (See *Tropical Rainforest Destruction*.)

CFCs

The destroyers of the ozone layer are also responsible for 14%[5] of the GE (40% in the US, over 50% in Japan)[3] with each CFC molecule trapping 10,000xs more heat than one of carbon dioxide.[5] (See *Depletion of Ozone Layer*.)

Methane

About 18% of the GE,[1] methane levels are growing at 1–2% per year and have doubled since pre-industrial times.[5] Methane has 25xs the GE of carbon dioxide,[3] and most comes from the digestive processes of cattle, microbes in paddy fields, coal mines, natural gas pipelines, the burning of industrial wastes, and landfill sites.

Nitrous oxides

About 6% of the GE,[1] nitrous oxide levels are steadily increasing. Nitrous oxide comes from fertilizers and the burning of fossil fuels in power stations and cars. (See *Acid Rain.*)

Ozone

Hydrocarbons (from cars, solvents, natural gas) and nitrous oxides (from cars and power stations) react in sunlight to form ozone, which is poisonous in the lower atmosphere and accounts for 12% of the GE.[1]

EFFECTS

Rising temperatures

In the last 100 years, the earth has warmed about 0.6° Celsius,[3] which may not sound much, but a drop of 4° Celcius is enough to bring on a full ice age.[5] And the 1980s (up to the end of 1988) saw the 5 hottest years since records began, 130 years ago.[1]

Even without more carbon dioxide emissions, a further 1° Celsius rise over the next few decades is already assured, making the earth warmer than since civilization began. Unchecked, we can expect a global rise of 1.5°–4.5° Celsius between 2030 and 2050, with little change at the Equator[2] but up to 7° Celsius at the Poles. In less than 100 years, it could be 8° warmer.

Rising sea levels

Since 1900, sea levels have risen 10–15 cm,[5] due to thermal expansion in the oceans and melting glaciers and ice caps. The permanent ice cap over the Arctic thinned from 6–7 m to 4–5 m between 1976 and 1987 in an area north of Greenland.[6] Scientists predict increased sea levels of as much as 1.65 m by 2030, and 2, perhaps 3.5, m by 2100.[5]

A 1 m rise could affect all land up to 5 m, risking 5 million sq km – only 3% of world area, but $\frac{1}{3}$ of global cropland and home to 1 billion,[3] threatening cities like New Orleans, Cairo, and Shanghai. Much of Asia's best rice land would be ruined; the Maldives, mostly 2 m or less above sea level, would be endangered. By 2030, flooding would put 1.3 million at risk in London, and adequate sea defences around Britain would cost about £8 billion.[5]

Weather

Climatic shifts could be abrupt, with agricultural losses not easily compensated for,[2] and extreme and freak weather conditions. Africa would be hit worst, with fuelwood disappearing and deserts advancing. The US, Central America, South-East Asia would suffer droughts. Places like the UK could become cooler as the Gulf Stream moved north. Small effects on the monsoon could affect 1+ billion in China, 1 billion in India, and millions elsewhere. Even now, we could be seeing the first major effects, with recent severe droughts in the American mid-west and China; record low temperatures in Alaska, Lebanon, Jordan; exceptionally mild winters in Western Europe, Scandinavia, USSR; and the highest rainfall for years in Australia.

Agriculture

Modern crops have a narrow range of temperature tolerance, so drier conditions in the major grain growing areas of North America, the USSR, and Central Europe could mean serious losses in world grain supplies. Climatic changes might appear to benefit Canada, Siberia, and Scandinavia, but their poorer soils would not compensate. With its massive grain exports reduced, US influence would decline. 1988 (the hottest year in 100 years) illustrates how hotter summers affect agriculture: causing the US grain harvest to fall below consumption for the first time, and grain losses of 97 million tons from the US, the USSR, and China.[3]

Famine

Famine will increase in dry parts of Africa, and drought in India particularly, with agriculture difficult to continue within 30 years (crops have failed 3 out of the last 4 years in Rajasthan).[7] Economies will be severely affected, with millions facing starvation and destruction of lifestyles; adapting will often be impossible.

Mass migrations and world security

The uprooting of 1 billion from India, plus millions more elsewhere, dislocated by coastal flooding, droughts, agricultural disruption, would have unimaginable effects, perhaps upsetting the whole balance of global security.

Wildlife

Effects on marine ecosystems are hard to predict; but the abruptness of the GE – within 60 years[8] – will cause many extinctions, as species fail to adapt. Northern forests, unable to cope with even small temperature changes and rainfall reductions, will be badly affected. Isolated remnants of wildlife in nature reserves will probably die out.[4] Possibly, the whole system could be pushed over the brink, leading to an uncontrollable chain reaction . . .

6

Other effects

Drinking water could be affected; with a possible shortfall in New York of up to 42% by 2050. Many rivers and lakes could shrink or dry up – the Great Lakes in Canada could fall by up to 8 feet.[4] Hydroelectric generation will be affected. Tropical diseases and parasites might move north; Europe could be subject to malaria epidemics.

Optimistic talk, then, like growing melons in Britain, is dangerous and irrelevant: the GE will yield no winners, only victims.

WHAT HAS BEEN DONE

Despite all this, politicians currently seem to favour adapting to, rather than preventing, the GE. And although rising higher on the political agenda, nothing concrete has yet been done.

- The November 1989 GE conference in Noordwijk in Holland agreed nothing more concrete than a freezing of developed world carbon dioxide emissions at present levels by 2000 and investigating the feasibility of a 20% reduction by 2005.
- At the February 1990 Washington UN International Panel on Climate Change (IPCC) meeting – to the dismay of the Western world – President Bush denied there was even a problem, and the Third World, not surprisingly, was nervous about taking steps that would limit development.
- Nevertheless, West Germany has pledged to cut carbon dioxide emissions by 25% by 2005; Holland to peg them at 1990 levels by 1995; and France, Italy, Denmark, and Norway to stabilize them by 2000. Mrs Thatcher, meanwhile, agreed to a pitiful pegging of 1990 emissions by 2005.
- The two May and June 1990 IPCC reports pronounced the GE as a major threat requiring immediate action; the third report, drawn up by politicians, (predictably) failed to produce any urgent recommendations. The US, together with Japan, the USSR, China (worried about impeding development), and Saudi Arabia (worried about oil markets) said they could not cut GE emissions quickly.

WHAT SHOULD BE DONE

The positive, but ironical, thing about the GE is that its very severity gives us hope, because it will also mean tackling many other major issues: tropical rainforest destruction, ozone depletion, energy (also a cause of acid rain), transport, habitat loss, even agriculture.

- Introduce a verifiable climate treaty similar to the Montreal Protocol for CFCs.

- Cut greenhouse gas emissions by over 60%, immediately, to stabilize concentrations at present levels, says the May 1990 IPCC report. The sooner it happens, the cheaper it will be, the less devastation done.

- Energy conservation is the *quickest*, *cheapest* way of reducing carbon dioxide emissions – 7 times more cost-effective than nuclear power: Britain could reduce mean electricity demand by 70%, providing the same services, 5–10xs cheaper.[9] In Canada, a 20% reduction in carbon dioxide emissions will cost $108 billion, but save $192 billion![3] (See *Energy*.)

- The developed world must help Third World industry develop with the cleanest, most efficient technology.

- Introduce gradually a carbon tax on fossil fuels, to restrain energy consumption and car use.

- Stop CFC production – the quickest, easiest measure available. (See *Depletion of Ozone Layer*.)

- Stop tropical deforestation; increase ecological afforestation (trees absorb carbon dioxide, turning it into wood as they grow). (See *TRF Destruction*.)

- Rein back road transport, which produces 20% of carbon dioxide in Britain (plus nitrous oxides).[10] (See *The Transport Problem*.)

- Trap methane, a useful energy source. (See *Energy*.)

- Limit fertilizer usage, which gives off nitrous oxides. (See *Agriculture*.)

- Conserve globally major natural stores of carbon – such as peat bogs, mature forests, and wetlands. (See *Habitat Loss*.)

WHAT YOU CAN DO

- Cut your share of energy demand. (See *Energy*.)
- Avoid all products containing CFCs. (See *Depletion of Ozone Layer*.)
- Buy cars with catalytic converters, and wherever possible walk, cycle, or use public transport (which are far less polluting and energy intensive.) (See *The Transport Problem*.)
- Don't buy tropical hardwood products unless they are from sustainable sources. (See *TRF Destruction*.)
- Write to your local politician; and join organizations like WWF, Friends of the Earth, Greenpeace, who are lobbying about the GE.

3
Depletion of the Ozone Layer

INTRODUCTION

The ozone layer, 12–30 miles above the earth, absorbs about 99% of the sun's damaging ultraviolet radiation (UV–B),[1] which would otherwise scorch life off the face of the earth. Yet at sea level (pressure), it would be no thicker than a pound coin.[2]

However, global ozone levels have dropped 5% in the last decade[3] and 8% across Europe and parts of North America in winter over the last 20 years.[4] Between Australia and Antarctica, they dropped a staggering 10% between 1986 and 1989, compared to a predicted 7% over 80 years![5] It is not known whether the atmosphere will reach a threshold and lurch into disaster.

CAUSES

CFCs and halons

These are responsible for 90% of the damage. Currently, we put out 6xs more than can be absorbed by the atmosphere, with some lasting over 100 years.[2]

In 1987, global CFC production was about 1 million tonnes, worth $2 billion, and dominated by about 24 companies in the US, Europe, and Japan.[6] The main producers were such multinational chemical companies as ICI, DuPont, Hoechst, and Autochem, with the UK being Europe's largest producer and exporter. China and India, with 33% of the world's population, use a mere 2%.[7]

In March 1989, 62% of UK CFC production went into aerosols.[8] Foam blowing for hamburger cartons, carpet underlay, car seats, polystyrene, and insulation was the next biggest market. Other major uses include air conditioners, refrigerants, fire extinguishers, and solvents in the computer industry.

10

Others

Carbon tetrachloride is increasing in the atmosphere at 1% per year, methyl chloroform at 7%.[9] The first is used for dry cleaning and crop fumigation; the second as a cleaning fluid and a solvent in typing correction fluid, for example. Both are powerful ozone eaters.

EFFECTS

Holes over the Poles

Since 1979, a hole in the ozone layer has appeared over Antarctica every September and October, with ozone levels over the South Pole diminishing 40%;[6] by 1987, it had expanded to twice the size of the continental US.[10] A smaller hole was found over the Arctic, centred over Spitsbergen in Norway in 1986; and in February 1989, the layer was found to be unexpectedly primed for destruction. In 1987, a hole appeared over Melbourne.

Effects on humans

A 1% reduction in ozone could cause an estimated 15,000 new skin cancers annually in the US[1] and 70,000 worldwide.[7] Already, cases of malignant melanoma have doubled in the last 10 years and are increasing by 5% a year globally. In 1989, 27,300 Americans suffered from skin cancer, 6,000 died from it.[11] In Australia, the incidence of skin cancer is up 500% in the last 20 years.[12] Cataracts and other eye diseases will increase, and genetic mutations are possible.

Effects on wildlife

An increase in UV–B threatens many lifeforms, especially ocean food chains, where plankton (the main food for fish and sea mammals such as whales, dolphins and so on, and an important element in oxygen production) and crustaceans, young fish, and larvae in clear water are especially sensitive.

11

Effects on agriculture

$\frac{1}{5}$ of crop species are extremely sensitive too, including members of the bean, cabbage, melon and squash families. A 15% reduction in ozone would reduce US corn, cotton, soyabean, and wheat harvests by an estimated $900 million.[9] Trees and grasses are vulnerable and wild and domestic animals could suffer skin cancer and eye defects.

Greenhouse Effect

And to cap it all, CFCs are responsible for between 14%[13] and 25% of the GE globally.[14] (See *The Greenhouse Effect*.)

WHAT HAS BEEN DONE

- Suspicions about CFCs emerged in 1974 from the US. In 1978, the US Environmental Protection Agency (EPA) banned them in aerosols. Canada followed suit.
- Only in 1985, with much attention on the Antarctic ozone hole, did the rest of the world take things seriously. In 1987, 46 nations signed the Montreal Protocol to reduce the use of 5 CFCs and 3 halons by 50% by 2000.
- At the March 1989 London Ozone Conference, attended by 124 nations, the US and EEC agreed a 100% phase out of Montreal Protocol gases by 2000. By July 1990, 59 nations had signed, with another 39 expected to do so soon.
- At the June 1990 London Ozone Conference (attended by 90 nations), it was agreed that all CFCs, halons, and carbon tetrachloride would be phased out by 2000, methyl chloroform by 2005. China and India now look like signing, with a fund agreed upon to help the Third World. 14 countries (Canada, New Zealand, Australia, and 11 European countries – Britain not included) agreed to phase out CFCs by 1997. Unfortunately, chemical companies plan to replace 30% of the CFC market with HCFCs, which are still damaging, although less so.[15]
- In Britain, due to a successful Friends of the Earth consumer boycott (the Government was irrelevant in this), the 8 leading aerosol manufacturers agreed to phase out CFC use by the end of 1989, so that now (in mid 1990), over 90% of aerosols are CFC free.[16]

- In 1987, Macdonalds said it would phase out CFC-containing food packaging.

WHAT SHOULD BE DONE

- Only an immediate 100% ban on CFCs and halons, plus controls on other ozone-depleting chemicals (carbon tetra-chloride and methyl chloroform) can stabilize ozone layers – that is the overwhelming consensus of scientists.

  A leading scientist warned of a possible 18% ozone depletion over the Northern Hemisphere during winter and spring by 2000; and at current levels of reduction it would be 2030 before ozone depleting chemicals went down to 1986 levels.[17]
- Legislation or fiscal incentives must be adopted to encourage safe recovery and recycling of CFC refrigerants and other ozone depleting chemicals. The developed world must help developing countries to meet needs without using these substances.

WHAT YOU CAN DO

- Buy only CFC-free ('Ozone Friendly') aerosols, and encourage family and friends to do the same.
- Don't buy other things containing CFCs – for advice, ask the shop assistant, or write to the manufacturer, or read John Elkington and Julia Hailes' *The Green Consumer Guide,* Gollancz, 1988.
- Buy new fridges and freezers only with reduced CFCs in the insulation and cooling system. Ask the manufacturer or local authority to dispose of the old one safely.
- In Britain, write to ICI, the biggest CFC manufacturer, asking when they will phase out ALL non-essential CFCs.
- Stop your school, college, local authority using CFC-containing products – a petition might be useful.

4

Tropical Rainforest Destruction

INTRODUCTION

Tropical rainforests (TRFs) are the richest habitats on earth, forming a green belt around the Equator, 20 degrees north and south, from South and Central America to West Africa to South-East Asia. While they cover only 8% of the earth's land area,[1] they contain more than 50% of all species.[2] They also anchor the earth's most important cycles like the soil, water, air – upon which man is totally dependent.

Deforestation has been going on for centuries, but losses accelerated in the 1950s, again in 1980,[3] and yet again in the late 1980s.[4] By 1988, half of the world's TRFs were gone[5] – currently destroyed or seriously degraded at a terrifying 200,000 sq km per year, an area the size of Nebraska or $\frac{4}{5}$ of Great Britain. At present accelerating rates of destruction, few accessible TRFs will be left by 2000.[2] This would represent one of the biggest ecological disasters ever; and is the key to other major environmental problems: mass extinctions, the GE, squandering of natural resources, and the elimination of tribal people.

CAUSES

Third World debt

powers deforestation. The Third World is being bled dry by massive interest repayments to the developed world. The quick-fix solution to pay these debts is to liquidate forests, fisheries, minerals, soils. (See *Rich World; Poor World.*)

The misguided policy of the World Bank

and other multilateral development banks has led to the clearance of vast areas of virgin forest to make way for grandiose and inappropriate 'development' projects, like dams in the Amazon and the Narmada Valley Development Project in

14

India (with over 3,000 dams, 30 of them large) – all paid for by our taxes. Multinationals do more of the same, with vast logging operations, plantations, and mining.

Commercial logging

accounts for 50,000 sq kms of deforestation annually, mostly in West Africa and South-East Asia.[6] 99.8% of tropical timber is from forests that are not sustainably harvested, with European and Japanese demand for cheap tropical hardwoods accelerating destruction. In 1986, Japan alone consumed 29% of the tropical timber trade,[7] mainly to make plywood concrete-mouldings for construction and for disposable chop-sticks. Vast areas of forest thus become 'plywoodized', used once, then thrown away.

Cattle ranching

to produce cheap beef to make US hamburgers, is responsible for most of the 66% of Central American TRF loss in the last 30 years.[6] The Amazon forest, the world's biggest TRF, is being burned to the ground for more of the same. At present rates, this pearl of natural wonders will be all but hamburgerized by 2000.[8]

Clearance for subsistence agriculture

is a major cause of destruction and is fuelled by population growth, inequitable land distribution, and the expansion of cash crops. This leads to growing numbers of landless peasants, who must clear forest simply to grow food.

Fuelwood collection

for cooking and warmth denudes vast areas of trees, especially around rapidly growing cities in Asia and Africa.

EFFECTS

Extinctions

TRF destruction is by far and away the most serious cause, leading to an estimated 1–50 species extinctions globally a day.[5] At present rates, 20% of all species will be gone by 2000 and a phenomenal 50% in the next 50 years.[9] This will have unpredictable, but certainly catastrophic, effects on life as we know it. (See *Extinctions.*)

Tribal people

200 million people, living in or near the TRFs, are dependent on them for fuel and food.[10] They are almost universally without rights, and persecuted.

Loss of non-wood resources

New research shows that TRFs are more valuable left standing. In a Peruvian TRF, the net present value (NPV) of sustainable fruit and latex collection was estimated at $6,330 per ha, whilst clear felling was worth a mere $1,000 per ha, and cattle ranching a meagre $148 per year before costs.[11]

Loss of potential medicines, crops, jobs

Many everyday products are derived from the TRFs – for example, rubber, bananas, pain-killers. 25% of medicines contain compounds from TRF plants. And the sap of the Amazonian tree, *Copaiba langsdorfia*, is so similar to diesel that it can be used unaltered in trucks. This potential cornucopia of new products is being hamburgerized and plywoodized out of existence before we know what we're losing.

Greenhouse Effect

TRF destruction is the second major cause of carbon dioxide emissions, the major GE gas.[12] (See *Greenhouse Effect.*)

Soil erosion

With the protection of the forest gone, the fragile, infertile jungle soils erode rapidly, forming gulleys and washing away nutrients. The land becomes infertile and unable to support farming, cattle ranching, plantations, or forest again. Deserts can follow. Siltation of dams, reservoirs, irrigation systems occurs downstream; at the coast, coral reefs are choked. With the forest gone, water flow becomes erratic, both floods and droughts increase, and rivers like the Ganges, Brahmaputra, Irrawady, Salween, and Mekong no longer supply constant irrigation water, and city water supplies are threatened.

Effects on global weather patterns

TRFs help regulate global weather patterns, so the destruction of the Amazon could effect the movement of moist air masses that regulate weather in North American farming areas. 1988's catastrophic US drought may portend far more serious and permanent changes.

WHAT HAS BEEN DONE

- 1989 saw international concern over the Amazon. The murder of Chico Mendes, Brazilian rubber tapper and ecologist, and the February meeting of Indians protesting the highly contentious Cararao Dam put Brazil in the international spotlight. In March, the World Bank withdrew its $500 million loan for the Cararao Dam and commercial banks scrapped a further $600 million. The new Brazilian president, Fernando Collor de Mellio, appears to want to save the Amazon. He invited Jose Lutzenburger, Brazil's best-known ecologist, to become environment secretary in March 1990; and he eliminated subsidies to ranchers, which had fuelled destruction before.
- In 1988, Thailand banned logging, as devastating floods in the south killed 350. The Philippines has banned raw timber exports.
- The World Bank and Third World governments have tentatively placed TRF preservation higher on the agenda and are encouraging reforestation as part of rural development.
- About 4% of tropical forests – an area 3xs the size of Britain, or a little bigger than Texas – are now guarded to some degree in 560 areas.[13] This needs to be trebled, but is at least a start.
- Friends of the Earth, Britain, are researching the possibility of a mega-debt swap, with the richest countries buying $50 billion of Brazil's debt at a discount price of $17 billion, in return for a verifiable programme of Amazon conservation. (See *Habitat Loss*.)
- The EEC, in 1989, announced important controls on its £5

17

billion tropical timber imports, to safeguard TRFs.

- The EEC is debating a carbon tax, to go towards saving the TRFs. Small charges would lead to large revenues.
- By late 1989, about 200 British retailers had stopped selling goods made from unsustainably-produced tropical hardwoods. And in West Germany, 150 towns and communities had banned TRF hardwoods.
- Due to a 1987 consumer boycott, US Burger King announced that they – the main culprits – would stop using Central American rainforest beef.

WHAT SHOULD BE DONE

- Prohibit all logging in virgin tropical forests; all timber must come from selectively logged secondary forest or plantations. Introduce an international labelling scheme for hardwoods.
- Currently, tree planting is a tiny 10% of destruction. 1.1 million sq km of new forests – an area 4xs the size of Great Britain – are needed by 2000 for fuelwood, for ecological stabilization, for combating the GE.[12] Species must be carefully chosen, as eucalyptus can drain water and nutrient reserves.
- Increase developed world aid (although not to the highly criticized Tropical Forestry Action Plan) to stop tropical deforestation and increase ecological afforestation.
- Brazil needs to reduce population growth and introduce proper land reform to save the Amazon.
- Introduce to the Third World wood-burning stoves, which are 50% more efficient.
- Import only sustainably-produced tropical timber into developed countries; place a 4% tax on these to finance the projects behind them.
- Reduce demand for tropical timber in developed countries by growing more wood and recycling more paper.

WHAT YOU CAN DO

- Boycott hamburgers that contain 'rainforest-beef' (British ones don't); likewise, Brazilian corned beef.
- Avoid furniture, doors, windows, etc made from unsustain-

ably-produced tropical hardwoods. In Britain, the Friends of the Earth *Good Wood Guide* can give you advice. Common tropical hardwoods include: iroko, keruing, mahogany, red, yellow, and white meranti, lauan, seraya, obeche, ramin, sapele, and teak.

- Support natural forest harvests by buying Brazil nuts and rubber products.
- Check whether your bank is funding destructive projects in TRFs (some British banks have done so in the past).
- Support environmental groups with TRF projects. (See *Useful Addresses*.)

5
Acid Rain

INTRODUCTION

Acid rain is a cocktail of acidic chemicals that is carried by the wind and delivered by the rain hundreds, even thousands, of miles from its origin. It was first linked with dying fish in Scandinavia as far back as 1959 and with the death of Germany's forests in 1980. Damaging or killing forests, lakes, wildlife, humans, buildings, works of art, acid rain is one of the most serious environmental threats in the Northern Hemisphere. It is worst in Europe and North America, with damage as far afield as Southern India, Brazil, Chile, Mexico, South-East Asia, Eastern China, and Australia. Tropical areas are especially vulnerable due to poor soils.[1]

CAUSES

Acidic emissions come from burning fossil fuels mainly in coal-and oil-fired power stations, industrial boilers, large smelters, and cars. British acid rain emissions are composed of 70% sulphur dioxide, about 30% nitrous oxides, and a touch of hydrocarbons.[2] These are then converted into sulphuric acid, nitric acid, ammonium sulphate, and ozone. The problem is massive. The US produces 26 million tonnes of sulphur dioxide and 22 million tonnes of nitrous oxides a year. Canada receives 50% of its acid rain from the US.[3]

Sulphur dioxide

Britain is the largest producer in Western Europe, with 70% coming from power stations.[4] It is also the largest polluter of other European nations, with 75% reaching predominantly: Southern Norway, Sweden, Denmark, Holland, Belgium, and West Germany.[1] In Norway, 96% comes from other countries![1] We now produce 60–70xs more per year in Europe than we did during the filthy years of the Industrial Revolution.

Nitrous oxides

Britain produces 40% from power stations, 40% from traffic.[2]

Ozone

Formed by hydrocarbons and nitrous oxides in sunlight, this is a secondary, but nevertheless important, pollutant. Ozone and acid pollution combined are the major cause of forest destruction in Central Europe.

EFFECTS

Between the 1950s and 1970s, rain in Britain and Europe became more than 10xs more acidic, with Britain's worst a pH 2.4 at Pitlochry in Scotland, as acidic as vinegar and 1,000xs more than natural.[2]

Damage to lakes

Plant nutrients are leached from the soil, and aluminium and heavy metals are activated, killing fish and contaminating water.

Tens of thousands of lakes are dead in Canada, the US, Sweden, Norway, and Eastern Europe,[4] with nearly $\frac{1}{2}$ the fish in Southern Norway dead and nearly $\frac{1}{4}$ of Swedish lakes acidified.[3] In the US, 3,000 lakes are marginally acidified, 1,000 are acidified,[2] 212 in the Adirondacks have no fish.[5] In Canada, in 1989, over 14,000 were strongly acidified, with 150,000 (1 in 7) in the east biologically damaged.[1] This is mirrored to a lesser extent in the rest of Europe, with 57 lakes in Scotland losing all their fish.[4]

Damage to forests

Leaves and roots are attacked, making trees vulnerable to frost, drought, poor drainage, pests and diseases – which usually kills them.

In North America, most damage so far is at high altitude. In China, damage is reported from the South-West. In Europe, 35% of forests are damaged[1] across 20 countries[2] and 500,000 sq km – an area slightly smaller than France.[1] Britain's trees are the most damaged after Denmark,[6] with fewer than 50% of forests healthy,[2] although recent reports (1990) from Czechoslovakia suggest 70% of trees have been 'influenced' by pollution![7] West Germany estimates costs of tree loss at about $2.98–4.77 billion annually for the next 70 years.

Damage to people

Globally, nearly 625 million people breathe unhealthy levels of sulphur dioxide.[1] In Southern Norway, high levels of aluminium in well-water are linked to high levels of Alzheimer's disease (senile dementia). In Britain, heart attacks claim 5–8,000 each year in acid-water towns; and lead, dissolved from water pipes by acidic water, is damaging the brains of hundreds of thousands of children.[2]

Damage to buildings and works of art

Across Europe, paintings, stained glass, cathedral stone, historic books, and monuments are being eaten up at record rates. Athenian monuments have eroded more in the last 20–25 years than in the previous 2,400.[1] St Paul's Cathedral in London has lost 2.5 cm of stonework in the last 100 years.[3] Annual building damage in London is estimated at £2–100 million; in Britain £16–770 million.[2] And in the US, statues and tablets at the Gettysburg Civil War battlefield are being slowly eaten away.[1]

Damage to wildlife

In Scandinavia and North America, ospreys and divers are declining due to lack of food.[8] In the British Peak District, acid tolerant cotton grass and bilberry are taking over from other species. 72% of suitable sites have no dippers in North Wales. Otter populations are restricted.[2] In the North of Britain, the introduced rhododendron takes over woodlands, suffocating all other plants; this acid-loving plant is poised to spread further with increasing acidity.

Damage to crops

In the US, the 1980s ozone levels led to an estimated 5%, perhaps 10%, yield loss, worth about $5.4 billion. Globally, this was an estimated 48 million tonnes for North America, Europe, and China in 1987.

Damage to coastal waters

Acid deposition is a major contributor to the degradation of America's Chesapeake Bay, accounting for 25% of nitrogen deposition. This is 27% for the Baltic Sea.[1] (See *Ocean Pollution.*)

Other

In the Katowice region in southern Poland, trains have to slow down in certain places, due to rail tracks corroded by acid rain.

WHAT HAS BEEN DONE

- The June 1989 revisions of the US 1970 Clean Air Act plan to reduce sulphur dioxide emissions from power stations by 50% by 2000. (See also *The Transport Problem.*) The Canadians are aiming at 25% by 1994.
- Western Europe has agreed a 30% reduction on 1980 levels by 1993 and 60% from major sources by 1995. This is the minimum we should aim at, and would cost the average British consumer a mere £2–3 per year.[4] And yet Britain, as always, dragged its heels, agreeing a weak compromise, and that only under threat of legal action from the European Commission; even this it looks set to break.
- West Germany, at least, is setting a good example, with a reduction of 24% between 1982 and 1986 and 80% aimed at for 1990 on large power stations.
- Between 1980 and 1985, Sweden spread 1 million tonnes of finely ground limestone into about 3,000 lakes at a cost of $30 million.[9] Useful as this may be as a stop-gap and clean-up measure, it is not particularly effective, has side effects, and is no substitute for prevention.
- Eastern Europe has yet to act.

WHAT SHOULD BE DONE

Compared to the cost of the damage, emission control starts to look cheap.

- Reduce sulphur dioxide emissions from power stations by a minimum of 80–90% and nitrous oxides by 75% (the least needed to protect sensitive habitats) as soon as technically possible,[10] but within 10 years.
- The cheapest means (and the main solution for the GE) is increased energy efficiency. (See *The Greenhouse Effect*; *Energy*.)
- Transfer Western technology to Eastern Europe and the Third World, to limit pollution as industrialization proceeds there – after all, we will all suffer from it.
- Build new power stations, as clean and efficient as possible.
- Rein back road transport. (See *The Transport Problem*.)

WHAT YOU CAN DO

- Cut your energy demand. (See *Energy*; *The Transport Problem*.)
- In Britain, write to the CEGB saying you're willing to pay the tiny £2–3 per year on your bill for them to clean up their power stations.[4] (See *Useful Addresses*.)
- Drive more slowly and turn off your engine when you stop – both cut pollution.
- Write to your local politician, asking for action to clean up cars and power stations.
- Ask your local paper to print an article about acid rain.
- Join, donate to, get involved in, environmental groups campaigning about acid rain – in Britain, WWF, Friends of the Earth, and Greenpeace.

6
Rich World; Poor World

INTRODUCTION

Third World poverty is one of the most important environmental issues, because it puts enormous pressures on environments, especially TRFs, grasslands, soil, fisheries.

In the last two centuries, the gap has widened between the rich and poor countries, with GNP per capita now 40xs less on average in the developing countries and 5–6xs less even in the fastest developing countries like Brazil.[1] The developed world, with only $\frac{1}{5}$ of world population, consumes $\frac{4}{5}$ of the world's resources[2] (the US, alone, devours $\frac{2}{5}$),[3] $\frac{4}{5}$ of energy, $\frac{2}{3}$ of income,[1] with nearly all technology originating there and most information created, stored, and distributed there.[1]

After some decades of improvement, the 1980s were one of negative development for the Third World. For the poor, especially in Africa and Latin America, diets deteriorated and death rates increased. 47 nations were probably poorer in per capita terms in 1990 than 1980, due to continuing environmental deterioration, exploding populations, slumping commodity prices, and multiplying debt.[4]

CAUSES

Third World poverty is caused by the factors listed below, each exacerbating the rest. Developed world affluence, on the other hand, is attributable to industrialization, climatic factors, cultural values, and colonialism, which milked Third World resources. Perhaps most importantly, the international economic system, designed by the rich in their own interests, is biased against the poor countries.

Inequality of income
Gross inequality of income is the norm in Third World

25

countries, characterized by a huge rural poor (maybe 75% of the population), a small urban middle class, and a tiny political elite. Many national policies neglect or discriminate against the poor, and unfair land distribution is rife. In Latin America (where it is worst), 88% of the land is owned by 6% of the population.[5]

Overconsumption in the West

In consuming $4/5$ of energy and resources,[1,2] the West doesn't leave much for the rest. If everyone had a Western standard of living, we'd need three planets to support us.

Third World debt

In the early 1970s, when interest rates were low, major Western banks loaned oil money to developing countries. Subsequently, recession (with plummeting Third World commodity prices) and higher interest rates have multiplied global debts from $60 billion to $1,200 billion between 1973 and 1989.[6,4]. Since 1984, as massive interest payments outstrip aid, huge transfers of money from poor to rich countries ($50 billion per year by 1988)[4] have occurred. Some countries pay 40–50% of their export earnings in repayment.[7] Thus, minerals, soils, grasslands, forests (ie the Amazon) are exploited, to pay debts. On top of this, landless populations overgraze fragile grasslands and overcut forests just to stay alive. Thus, the debt crisis fuels environmental destruction and makes real development impossible.

Inappropriate development

Despite over 30 years of Third World development, the numbers of poor are steadily rising, with almost 20% of humanity unable to achieve even the most meagre existence. Brazil, a leader in development, needs 362 years to equal rich world incomes, poor Mauritania needs 3,224![1] This is due to the pursuit of high-growth, export-oriented economies, encouraged by, and benefiting, Western banks and contractors, Western-backed dictators and their elite minorities; meanwhile, most of the population lack the most basic living standards. According to the 'trickle-down theory' of aid, the poor are *supposed* to benefit from grandiose projects, thus dams, power stations, roads, take precedence over clean water, self-sufficiency in food and fuelwood, basic health programmes, education, and adequate housing.

Trade barriers

Developed-country trade barriers cost the Third World an estimated $50–100 billion each year in lost sales and depressed prices. EEC tariffs for cloth are 4xs as high against poor countries as rich ones.

Capital flight

National elites bank their fortunes in foreign countries, with capital flight from Latin America amounting to $250 billion by late 1987. Venezuelan overseas holdings are $58 billion; its national debt $37 billion![4]

Military spending

Arms spending is nearly always a major impediment to development, especially in Africa. An estimated 20% of debt in non-oil developing countries, between 1972 and 1982, came from arms imports.[8] Furthermore, every dollar on military spending is one less available for food, water, sanitation, health, education, welfare. The equivalent of 2 weeks global military spending would provide adequate food, water, education, health, and housing for everyone in the world for a whole year.[9] (See *The Arms Race*.)

EFFECTS

By 1989, 1.2 billion lived in absolute poverty – $\frac{4}{5}$ were rural dwellers.[4] Much of the following catalogue of Third World suffering could be avoided with minor adjustments to budgets.

Food

Almost 500 million are undernourished,[1] with 40 million dying each year of starvation or hunger-related diseases[7] – the equivalent of 300 Jumbo jet crashes per day, almost half the passengers children, no survivors. Meanwhile, in Europe, a cat eats more meat than many people in the Third World.[1]

Worse still, this looks set to deteriorate, with a worldwide decrease in per capita grain production since 1984. Diets are deteriorating in Africa and Latin America, world grain prices have increased in the last two years, and world grain reserves are low. Environmental degradation is cutting global grain production by nearly 1% a year, and population is outstripping extra food production by about 2%:1%. Potential sources of extra food are nearly exhausted: extra land, fertilizer, irrigation, high-yielding varieties, yields themselves. Is mass Third World famine looming on the horizon?[4]

But despite all this, the earth could meet everyone's food and fuelwood needs indefinitely if properly managed.[1] So why the starving masses?:

The meat-rich diet of the West □ About 40% of the world's grain is fed to livestock to supply the meat-rich diet of the developed world,[1] with Europe importing 14 million tonnes of Third World crops each year, including from Ethiopia![10] Grain consumed directly by humans can support 10xs more people.

Cash crops □ The Third World should be self-sufficient in food, but this is not easy when much land is used to grow livestock feed, coffee, cocoa, tobacco, bananas, etc for export. When local people cannot be fed, development is slowed. And even if the local farmers, rather than the rich, own the land, they don't much benefit as they get a tiny slice of the cake and are susceptible to fickle prices.

The tragedy of the poor □ Lacking decent land or jobs, millions are forced to scrape a living out of marginal land, turning fields into desert and destroying forests – not out of ignorance, but necessity. National and international economic reforms are needed to give the underclass a living without destroying the environment.

Fuelwood

Most rural people have only one energy source: wood. And many countries have severe shortages (notably Sub-Saharan Africa), with wood cut at unsustainable levels and 1.5 billion having difficulty finding enough for cooking and heating,[1] especially around big cities. India's forest, for example, declined from 16.9–14.1% of land area between the early 1970s and early 1980s; as far back as 1982, forests could sustainably produce only 30% of demand.[11] Trees in the Third World need to be planted 5xs faster on average, 15–50xs in the worst areas.

Water

Provision of clean water and sanitation are urgent problems; ponds and rivers – the main source of water – are also used as toilets. Well over 50% of people, China excepted, are without plentiful clean water and 75% without sanitation. In rural areas, where hardship is the norm, the figures rise to 70% and almost 90% respectively. Unclean water kills 25 million each year, 15 million of them children, mostly from diarrhoea.

Health

High mortality rates, especially among children, are the norm in many countries. Up to age 5, 1 in 6 die; disability and illness then affect another $\frac{1}{3}$ of the population. Health care is often only available in towns; health workers, immunization, drugs, sanitation, and information are lacking; 800 million are without access to medical services.[1] Not surprising, really, when about 70–85% of public spending goes to expensive curative care,[4] unavailable to the poor majority. Many are trapped in a vicious circle: poor sanitation causes diarrhoea, which aggravates malnutrition, sapping energy and earning capacity, lowering the ability to put food on the plate: which weakens further, and lowers immunity against further illness . . .

Education

Education boomed in the 1960s and early 1970s, with the number of children in primary and secondary education almost tripling in 20 years. But illiteracy is still high: 74% in Africa, 47% in Asia, 24% in Latin America. In 1980, of 70% of children enrolled for primary school, only 61% completed four years; 120 million had no school to attend. Illness, the need to work, and high costs further depleted attendance rates. Illiterate people are usually poor, hungry, and vulnerable to disease and exploitation.

Other problem areas

The growing numbers of refugees – 8 to 12 million in the Third World – overstretch meagre resources. And rural communities are sapped of youngsters as they head hopefully for the exploding cities.[1]

WHAT HAS BEEN DONE

Things have not happened very quickly yet; but improving East–West relations could release massive resources, previously used in conflict, hopefully for use in the Third World.

- Canada has already cancelled $581 million of official debt owed by African countries. And the US plans to absolve 10 African countries of about $305 million.
- The Drinking Water and Sanitation Decade, 1981–1990, intended to supply the most basic services to more than 1 billion, was an inspired hope, and did focus governments' attention on their people's needs.
- South Korea is the only developing country to reverse the trend against deforestation. China is planning a 7,000 km forest belt covering a massive 2 million sq km. And India recently planned to plant 50,000 sq km each year, but is not yet close to this.
- Most countries committed to rural development have implemented land reforms, notably, China, Taiwan, Cuba, and South Korea.
- Although no substitute for fundamental change, hundreds of thousands of grass-roots groups have formed around the Third World, especially in the 1980s, helping hundreds of millions get what official development has failed to provide.
- The Indian state of Kerala has been putting the poor first for decades: the provision of health care, transportation, and education in that state is unprecedented elsewhere in India. Elements of its success are: literacy, which leads to higher incomes; improved health, and smaller families; secure land rights; local control over common resources; credit, which allows the purchase of livestock and tools etc; clean drinking water; primary health care; family planning; grass-roots organizations.[4]

WHAT SHOULD BE DONE

Fundamental reforms to the international order are needed; which means the rich countries must help the poor, only thus can Third World environments, upon which we all depend, be saved.

From the outside

Debt □ Debt relief, in exchange for policy reforms to help the poor and the environment, is urgently needed. To restore economic progress, debt must be cancelled in the very poorest countries, halved in other major debtor nations.[12]

Development □ Increase developed-world aid to at least 0.7% of GNP.[13] Development programmes must be environmentally sustainable, sensitive to tribal people, have the full involvement of local communities. The World Bank, the IMF, the aid agencies must put the basics first.

Trade restrictions and capital flight □ Developed world trade restrictions against poor countries must be lowered; capital flight from developing countries must be prevented.

From the inside

General environmental measures □ Population control, deforestation, soil erosion, energy efficiency and renewables must be at the top of the list. Industrialization must be selective, with the West helping install the best technology, so that economies could expand 10xs without using more energy (or producing more carbon dioxide).[14]

Agriculture □ Decentralized, agriculturally-based development, based on all-round self-sufficiency, is necessary to eradicate poverty. Agriculture should be organic, labour intensive, soil-conserving, and based on renewable energy. Cash crops must be cut. Land reform is vital to favour small farmers over commercial landowners. 'Only' $8 billion per year is needed to lift Third World peasant farmers out of poverty, compared to about $40 billion US farmers receive each year in subsidies.[1] (See *Agriculture*.)

31

Fuelwood □ 550,000 sq km of high-yielding fuelwood plantations (5xs present planting) and 1,000,000 sq km of forest for ecological rehabilitation are needed by 2000.[11]

Health □ Links are needed between the often urban-based medical community and rural populations. This need not be expensive: it costs only $5 per child to prevent the diarrhoeal diseases that claim 15 million each year.[1]

Water □ Clean water and hygienic toilet facilities are needed for everybody: this would save a lot of unnecessary illness and suffering.

Transport □ The bike is the ideal transport medium for Third World countries. It can provide a travel capacity at least 5xs that of walking, with huge potential benefits especially in Latin America, and Africa. With a trailer behind, 200 kg can be carried – saving much hard work.[4]

Education □ As female literacy rises, so do incomes, nutrition levels, and child survival rates; population growth slows.

WHAT YOU CAN DO

- Join an aid organization (See *Useful Addresses*). £10 donated will buy a medical kit for a health worker in Pakistan. £50 will immunize 16 children against six killer diseases.[15] £230 pays for a handpump in Cambodia.[16]
- Buy gifts and products from organizations involved in co-operative ventures: in Britain, Traidcraft and Oxfam.

7

The Population Bomb

INTRODUCTION

In 1990, the world population was 5.3 billion,[1] and set to increase by a probable average of 96 million per year during the 1990s (the equivalent of the populations of the UK, Belgium, Denmark, Ireland, Norway, Sweden, and Austria added together).[2] World population growth was about 1.65% in 1987, declining – but not fast enough – from an all-time high of about 2% in 1970.[3] It is growing exponentially and is expected to reach 6.25 billion by 2000 and nearly 9 billion by 2030,[2] reaching zero growth early in the 22nd century.[4] 95% of this increase will be in the Third World.[5]

This decline is so slow because: 1) Zero Population Growth (ZPG) is only reached when Death Rates (DRs) equal Birth Rates (BRs). 2) Third World populations are youth-heavy so even at replacement level (2.1 children per family), BRs exceed DRs. 3) At this stage – and most countries haven't reached it yet – it still takes 60 years for the youth-heavy population to come through the system.

Falls in BRs are, however, astounding in Japan and very marked in China, India, and Indonesia. The US should achieve ZPG within 40 years, Europe and the USSR tend towards ZPG, and West Germany is actually declining in numbers.[6] Unfortunately, though, most people live in the Third World, which often has very high growth rates – at its worst in Sub-Saharan Africa, where many countries show no decline in BRs and some average 6 or 7 children per family.[3]

CAUSES

In the Third World, advances in health led to very high population growth: DRs dropped dramatically, whilst BRs remained at previous high levels; Family Planning (FP) lagged way behind.

33

Social conditions

A combination of social conditions make population control difficult. These include:

- Most significantly, the low status of women and high illiteracy, low wages, and ill health that accompany it. In Africa, a woman's status rises with the number of children she bears, particularly as this means help with her grossly unfair burden of chores – farming, marketing, etc.
- Poverty, high infant mortality, and absence of social welfare mean more births to ensure enough survive to work for family income and care for parents in old age.
- Religion often favours large families. And in some countries, the number of children a man fathers enhances his status as a male. Many men have negative ideas about contraception – some educated Kenyan men believe condoms cause impotence; it is not uncommon for men to forbid wives to use contraceptives. Further, some cultures and some religious systems are prejudiced against contraception.

Lack of family planning

Only 27% of women in developing countries use FP, yet $\frac{1}{2}$ (China excepted) want no more children.[3] Contraception is unavailable, inaccessible, inappropriate for many. Furthermore, FP programmes succeed only when countries are culturally, socially and economically ready.

EFFECTS

The environment

Overpopulation exacerbates all other problems, and if not brought under control, will make curbing Greenhouse emissions to needed levels almost impossible.

Forests □ Forests are usually first to be affected, with 1.2 billion people in 1980 meeting fuelwood needs only by cutting wood faster than it grew.[3] As forest disappears, women and children spend more time collecting less wood. In parts of the Andes and the African Sahel, scarcity of fuel means only one hot meal a day. In India, cow dung and crop residues are used as fuel, compromising soil fertility.

Grasslands □ Livestock numbers multiply with human numbers, so fodder needs in most of the Third World now exceed the sustainable yield of grasslands and other forage,[3] leading to emaciated cattle, mass cattle deaths in droughts, widespread erosion.

Croplands □ Population growth and inequitable land distribution force landless farmers on to marginal land, incapable of long-term cultivation and easily eroded. Also, fallow cycles are shortened and crop rotations become ecologically unsound.

Desertification

This is often an end result, converting once-fertile land to desert. Worldwide, this happens to an area about the size of 7 Belgiums, or of Nebraska, each year.[7] (See *Desertification*.)

Famine

Land degradation lowers food production, which is one reason why the mid-1970s global per capita food production has not been improved upon. In Africa, per capita grain output has fallen by $\frac{1}{5}$ since 1970,[3] and, as we have seen, worldwide it has decreased since 1984, with diets deteriorating in Africa and Latin America.[2] Without massive land restoration and population control, in Africa especially, recurring famine will give way to chronic famine. (See *Rich World; Poor World*.)

Health

Lower food production leads to malnourishment, undernourishment and poor health. 40 million die each year from starvation and hunger-related diseases[8] – 17 million are children under 5.[9] (See *Rich World; Poor World*.)

Pressure on social and economic programmes

In many countries, population growth undermines programmes to improve diet, health, education. By 2000, 1.7 billion will be living in countries unable to support existing populations.[4]

Urbanization

Every day, about 75,000 rural poor, attracted by work and

prospects of a better life (usually neither exist), flood into overcrowded and overtaxed cities, mostly ending up in the shanty towns that house 75% in cities like Ibadan (Nigeria) and 67% in Calcutta.[4]

On habitats and wildlife

Population pressures for more agricultural land endanger habitats all over the Third World. In places like Kenya, the big game parks are threatened. Some ecologists, however, question the concept of game parks, as big game can – and for centuries did – thrive alongside local communities.

WHAT HAS BEEN DONE

Encouraging small families requires social change, backed up by FP. Few countries have either high on the agenda. Improvements globally are depressing, with half the world still above replacement level. However, some achievements stand out:

- China's controversial One-Child programme began in 1979, offering incentives and disincentives to keep family size to one. By 1987, the average was 2.4, a 56% decrease since the 1960s.
- In India, between 1960 and 1987, the fertility rate dropped 31% to an average of 4.3 children per woman. But by 2020 the population could still rise to about 1.3 billion, overtaking China as the most populous country.[3]
- In Thailand, mixing small-family incentives with programmes to increase community self-sufficiency rapidly accelerated contraception.
- Singapore, Cuba, Taiwan, and South Korea have reached or gone below replacement level. Chile, Colombia, and Costa Rica have cut birth rates by more than 50%. Brazil, Indonesia, and Mexico have made significant decreases.
- In Mexico, from 1972 to 1984, for every peso spent on FP, 9 were saved on maternal and infant health care, giving colossal net savings of $1.4 billion.
- Some new, injectable contraceptives – seen as more appropriate, as many women forget to take the pill[3] – are now in use in Third World countries.

36

WHAT SHOULD BE DONE

Reducing fertility needs the attention of the whole world – NOW.

- Basic reforms are needed to remove the conditions behind high fertility – notably poverty. Critical are the improvement of the status of women, infant survival, social services, employment, incomes, and education (the more schooling, the fewer children women have – since they have options beyond childbearing).
- Increase global FP expenditures from $2.5–7 billion per year over the next decade to achieve population stabilization at 8 rather than 10 billion by 2100.[3] Providing unmet FP needs is often the quickest and cheapest way to help the environment.
- Match contraceptives to the lifestyle, tastes, and pockets of the users. Find new approaches to marketing and distribution, for instance those relying on local residents and shopkeepers.[3] Introduce incentives and disincentives aimed at small families.
- Food shortages could be mitigated by good land use and limiting cash crops, measures desperately needed anyway.
- After population stabilization, gradually decrease world population to levels that can be supported sustainably.

WHAT YOU CAN DO

- Think seriously before having more than 2 children, as this increases the human population, which can only be at the expense of the environment.

8
Extinctions

INTRODUCTION

After humans appeared, extinction rates increased, until by the late 1980s – with massive tropical rainforest (TRF) destruction – they had soared to somewhere between 1 and 50 species a DAY.[1] This is accelerating, so 20% of wild species may be gone by 2000 (1,000xs the natural rate of extinctions[2]), more than 50% in 50 years[3] – representing the greatest biological destruction since life began, massively exceeding the great dying of the dinosaurs 65 million years ago.

Man depends on the 5–10 million species, thought to exist, for a huge range of services, many essential. Each extinction is like a thread pulled from the tapestry of life: you can remove a fair number without appearing to affect it, then whole sections fall apart.[3]

CAUSES AND EFFECTS

Habitat destruction

This is the main cause of extinctions and the one that essentially threatens the Californian condor, the mountain gorilla, and many other species. It is at its most frightening with the destruction of the TRFs – home to at least 50% of all species.[1] (See *TRF Destruction*.)

In Britain, massive habitat loss threatens 36 species of birds,[4] almost 1,800 of insects,[5] 10 butterflies, 317 plants,[4] and 20% of freshwater fish.[6] (See *Habitat Loss*.)

Agriculture

Apart from being responsible for massive habitat loss, the wholesale use of chemicals kills off all sensitive plants and animals from farmland the world over. (See *Inland Pollution*.)

Overexploitation

Overfishing □ In 1950, the world seafish harvest was 21 million tonnes; by the early 1970s it had soared to over 70 million, but failed to rise significantly due to mismanagement and overfishing. The 1960s and 1970s saw a general reduction of stocks,[7] with many fisheries collapsing, some spectacularly, like the Californian sardine fishery whose catch plummeted from 750,000 to 17 tons between 1936 and 1957.[8] Like many others, it never recovered.

Whaling □ Successive populations have been overexploited since Victorian times. Improved technology, soaring demand, no management strategy have driven many species towards extinction, with about 2 million whales killed this century,[9] reducing global populations 80–90%![10] The blue whale population crashed from perhaps 250,000 a century ago, to between 200 and 1,100 in 1989 – and is unlikely to survive.[11]

The wildlife trade

The fur business □ Big cats are especially exploited for their beautiful coats, with the chinchilla and ocelot vanishing from parts of Latin America. Clubbing baby seals in Canada has been largely stopped by the hard work of IFAW, but now a Taiwanese businessman plans to club 30,000 South African seals and turn them into dog food and aphrodisiacs. Once again, huge numbers of innocent animals are sacrificed on the altar of one man's profits.[12]

Africa's big game □ All big game in the Central Belt of Africa is threatened with extinction by 2000 from poaching, habitat loss, and overhunting. The African elephant, poached at 75,000 per year, has plummeted from 1.3 million in 1979 to 500,000 in 1989.[13] The black rhino is down from 65,000 in the late 1960s to fewer than 3,500 in 1989.[14] And the northern white rhino is down to 12.[15] Likewise, major game in India, South-East Asia, North America, Europe, and Central Asia is severely depleted.

Collectors □ Thousands of animals, especially monkeys, are taken for animal experiments. (See *Animal Abuse.*) Zoos, often buying from unscrupulous dealers, threaten other animals.

The pet business ☐ Millions of fish, reptiles, birds, and plants are taken for collectors and the pet trade. In 1979, about 250 million live fish and 4+ million reptiles (just the legal number) were imported into the US alone.[8]

Other ☐ Crocodiles, alligators, and snakes are hunted and killed to make handbags and shoes. Giant turtles are endangered for their shells. Over $\frac{1}{3}$ of European bird species are threatened over much of their range, with hunters in the Mediterranean illegally killing about 900 million per year – 1 in 7 UK migrants end up in a pot![60]

Predator control

The grizzly bear and the wolf have been exterminated over much of the US and Europe. Eagles are taken by gamekeepers. The Thylacene wolf of Tasmania is extinct. Fishermen kill ocean mammals as predators, from grey seals in the Orkneys to dolphins off Japan.

Introductions

Island ecologies are vulnerable to introductions due to their lack of defences. Hawaiian plants lack the aromas and spines to deter herbivores, so introduced grazing animals have caused many extinctions. The native wildlife of New Zealand and Australia has been ravaged by imported plants and animals. And in England the introduced grey squirrel has killed off the native red from large areas.

Others

In the USSR, poaching on reserves is rampant. In Australia, 3 million kangaroos are killed each year, with little evidence they do widespread damage.[16] Thousands of European frogs, toads, hedgehogs, badgers, deer are killed on the roads. And possibly as many as 500,000 small whales and dolphins are killed each year,[17] taken in tuna nets, snared in lost nets, killed for meat, polluted, and threatened by overfishing.

WHAT HAS BEEN DONE

Reserves

Theoretically, a world system of 'Biosphere Reserves' is being organized, but it may be too little too late.

The wildlife trade

The Convention on International Trade in Endangered Species (CITES), adopted by over 80 nations since 1973, deals with the illegal trade in threatened species and has delayed some extinctions.

Baby seal hunting

In June 1989, the EEC banned the import of Canadian baby harp and hooded seals indefinitely, replacing the 1983 ban which had successfully reduced demand by almost 75%.[11]

Overfishing

Successes are limited, but fisheries planning is improving, and there are new moves to protect marine environments, and new conventions and treaties.

Whaling

Following public concern, commercial whaling was temporarily banned worldwide in 1986; however Japan and Norway continued under the cynical label of 'scientific' whaling, although taking far fewer whales and no endangered stocks. Iceland agreed in 1989, after a consumer boycott, to stop until the end of 1990.

But Iceland, along with Japan and Norway, tried unsuccessfully to secure quotas for hunting at the July 1990 IWC (International Whaling Commission) meeting, where the ban on whaling was extended for another year.

The International Whaling Commission (IWC) are also considering protecting dolphins, porpoises, and small whales.

African big game

The October 1989 CITES conference introduced a two year ban on ivory trading, to be followed by strict regulation, confined to culling managed herds. Then in January 1990, Britain stunned environmentalists by giving Hong Kong, with the world's largest stockpile, a temporary exemption to clear stocks, thus seriously undermining the ban. By mid 1990, however, the ban had caused ivory prices to slump and poaching to decrease in some African countries – but it was too early for a full assessment.

Ranching

Ranching has the potential for conserving many wild animals, especially African big game. Ranched in East Africa, the oryx needs 5% of the water cattle do, matures quicker, has more calves, and, in semi-arid conditions, is more profitable.[7]

Wildlife tourism

About 10% of Kenya is wildlife reserves, being the largest foreign exchange earner at £180 million in 1987 and presenting a strong economic case for conserving wildlife.[15] But much of this money goes out of the country and local people derive few benefits. With political reforms, however, as discussed earlier, local people could be the beneficiaries.

Farming

Capybara are farmed in Venezuela, crocodiles in Thailand, vicuna in Peru, and butterflies in Papua New Guinea.

Specific projects

Hunting and poaching reduced the tiger population from 100,000 in the late 1930s, to 4,000 in 1970. But WWF's Operation Tiger has brought them back to 7,500 and their numbers are still increasing.[15]

WHAT SHOULD BE DONE

Parks and reserves

Although not enough on their own, triple the global area.[7]

Captive breeding

So many species are threatened that it is only practical to save them in the wild.

Global species census

Undertake a global species census to find out what is at risk and what undiscovered species exist, especially those with potential for medicines and crops.[18]

Treaties

Introduce more treaties, particularly covering migrating birds in Africa, Asia, and Europe; critical habitats; and endangered species.

CITES

Increase penalties and improve policing worldwide.

Fishing

Introduce stringent catch quotas, minimum net-mesh sizes, laws to protect dolphins, small whales, seals, etc. But most importantly, draw up an overall management plan for the oceans.[7]

Whales

Ban whaling globally, immediately, for ever.

African big game

Legislate the markets of ivory, horn, skin, etc in importing countries. Allocate far more money for poaching prevention in Africa. Place more emphasis on big game as an economic asset, especially to help local people.

WHAT YOU CAN DO

- Avoid being photographed with a chimp when holidaying in places like Spain; it may seem innocent enough, but for each animal arriving in Spain, 7 die in the barbaric process of capture and transport.[19] (See *Animal Abuse*.)
- Boycott ivory, whale products, the skins of cats and non-farmed animals, and other products that endanger wild populations. Without markets, there'd be no killing.
- To help the African elephant, please send donations to WWF Elephant Appeal. (See *Useful Addresses*.)
- Buy Dolphin-Friendly tuna. In Britain: only Sainsbury's 'Southseas' and 'Skipjack' tuna. In the US: Heinz (Star-Kist), VanCamp seafood (Chicken of the Sea), and BumbleBee Seafoods.
- In Britain (for example), do not pick or dig up wildflowers – if everyone did, soon there would be none.

9
Habitat Loss

INTRODUCTION

Humankind is destroying habitats at horrific rates, so that nearly every type, in every corner of the globe, is shrinking or being degraded, from forests to coral reefs, moorlands to mangroves, prairies to wetlands.

Apart from annihilating TRFs, we're doing a very effective job on coral reefs, mangroves, estuaries, and wetlands, all highly productive, with American east coast estuaries feeding the young of 95–98% of commercial fish species.[1] As far back as 1970, 23% of US estuaries were severely degraded, another 50% moderately so, with destruction at 0.5–1% of the total each year. Global figures are similar.[2]

In America and Canada, clear-cutting of virgin forests still progresses, subsidized by governments.

Antarctica, the world's only remaining pristine area, faces total degradation through potential mineral exploitation. Environmental destruction has already begun. The January 1989 sinking of an Argentinian supply ship – carrying 250,000 gallons of diesel – killed krill (the basic link of the food chain) in massive numbers, and contaminated seabirds with oil. The building of a runway at the French base of Dumont d'Urville, a flagrant abuse of internationally-agreed rules, threatens colonies of seabirds.

Farming, grazing, and the invasion of exotic plants have reduced to less than 0.1% the nearly 3 million sq km of tallgrass prairies that once covered the Midwestern US.[3]

Habitats are disappearing at ever increasing rates in Europe due to the EEC's farming and regionalization policy. In Britain, the story is grim. Since the late 1940s, destruction includes: 40% of deciduous woodland, 25% or 140,000 miles of hedgerows (enough to stretch almost 6xs around the Equator!),[4] over 50% of heathland,[5] 95% of wildflower-rich meadows,[6] 50% of lowland fen,[7] 80% of chalk and limestone grasslands, 33% of heather moorland, and 50% of river meadows and coastal marshes.[8]

CAUSES AND EFFECTS

TRF destruction □ is the most serious form of habitat loss with 50% already gone,[9] and a further 200,000 sq kms cleared or seriously degraded each year.[10] (See *TRF Destruction*; *Extinctions*.)

Third World debt □ with its massive interest payments, induces many developing countries to find the money by over-exploiting forests, fisheries, grazing lands, and soil. (See *Rich World; Poor World*.)

Agriculture □ with its monocultures of plants that support little wildlife, has eradicated plant communities all over the world, for example the Mediterranean area, now reduced to a 'goatscape'. Each year, more habitats are cleared for more farmland. Furthermore, the ubiquitous use of agricultural sprays contaminates waterways, kills all sensitive wildlife, and pollutes the environment wholescale. (See *Agriculture*; *Inland Pollution*.)

Urbanization □ wipes out entire habitats and tends to occur in biologically rich areas. In Britain, since 1949, an area the size of Berkshire, Buckinghamshire, Oxfordshire, and Bedfordshire, has been lost under concrete,[7] with developers given a free rein in the last 10 years. Furthermore, pipelines and roads fragment habitats and hinder migrations, with European frogs, toads, and salamanders killed in their millions on roads.

Desertification □ wipes out everything. (See *Desertification*.)

Pollution □ is now recorded in the deepest ocean trenches and the Antarctic ice. The Illinois river system, once a wildlife wonderland, is now a dead, stinking mess.[11] Estuaries and continental shelves are increasingly polluted. Acid rain is killing off lakes and forests *en masse*. Ozone depletion and the GE threaten calamitous effects. (See *Ocean Pollution*; *Acid Rain*; *Depletion of Ozone Layer*; *The Greenhouse Effect*.)

Big business □ In the Canadian state of Alberta, alone, public forest almost the size of Britain will be eliminated to fuel massive pulp mill projects as the government leases it to a dozen firms, despite plummeting prices.

Landfill □ (the disposing of domestic waste) destroys many valuable habitats, such as estuaries and old gravel pits. (See *Overconsumption*.)

Mining □ Open-cast mining destroys everything, and mining water from old tailings can exterminate all life.

Oil spillage □ kills wildlife in massive numbers. (See *Ocean Pollution*.)

Damming □ rivers, for hydroelectric projects, floods whole areas – destroying, in the tropics, millions of ha of TRFs, and displacing countless people.

Recreation □ In Britain, paths are severely eroded in the overvisited national parks. In the tropics, coral reefs are damaged by pleasure boat propellers and anchors and scuba diver fins. And in the south-west US, off-the-road vehicles degrade phenomenal amounts of desert with their lugged tyres.

The bomb □ War is an effective destroyer of habitats and nuclear weapons have the power to wipe life off the face of the earth. (See *The Arms Race*.)

WHAT HAS BEEN DONE

- 4.25 million sq km (about 1.75% of global land area) in about 3,500 areas worldwide are variously protected.[3] Costa Rica, a fine example, is 10% national parks.
- Bolivia was the first developing country to protect habitats in return for a debt swap (environmental groups buy bad debts from commercial banks, which in return retrieve at least some hard currency). Other countries have followed suit, with huge potential throughout the tropics.
- Some impressive reforestation schemes are planned in the Third World (See *Rich World; Poor World*), and the developed world alike. In the US, between 1985 and 1990, about 13 million ha of grass and trees were planted to curb

soil erosion and surplus production. And the Australians plan to plant 1 billion trees in the 1990s, replacing $\frac{1}{2}$ the tree cover lost since European arrival.

- At the 15th Antarctic Treaty conference, in October 1989, France and Australia proposed turning Antarctica into a nature reserve. No agreement was reached, as Britain (as usual, blocking any meaningful initiatives) and the US refused to accept. The USSR, Italy, Belgium, Spain, Germany, India, and New Zealand are all now leaning towards the Australian/French stance.
- The proposed EC Habitats Directive requires every country to establish Special Protection Areas (SPAs) to preserve the Community's most threatened habitats, plants, and animals. It is of course being watered down by Britain.
- In Britain, the Countryside and Forestry Commissions want to plant 'Community Forests' (each about 5,000 ha: $\frac{1}{2}$–$\frac{2}{3}$ for trees, the rest for recreation) around every major town and city by 2000. The programme, though, is not guaranteed success, as it relies on voluntary subscription of private land.

WHAT SHOULD BE DONE

In developed nations, stop further habitat loss and make all towns more hospitable to wildlife (and humans!) by planting millions of trees. In the Third World, the rich nations must help solve poverty, otherwise continued destruction seems inevitable. Longer-term, we need a worldwide reconstruction of lost habitats and wildlife.

- Triple the size of our present network of parks. In the Third World, they must meet the real needs of the people.
- 1 million sq kms of forest is needed in the developing countries by 2000, to replace lost habitats.[3]
- Establish Antarctica as a World Park.
- In the EEC, increase support for traditional forest management (eg parks and coppice in the UK, chestnut groves in the Pyrenees, cork oak in Greece). New planting should be with native species.[12]
- In Britain, give statutory protection to all Sites of Special Scientific Interest (SSSIs – some of the country's best habitats) and introduce planning controls for agriculture, forestry, and the water industry.

WHAT YOU CAN DO

- Support WWF's rainforest projects. Join Friends of the Earth who lobby for rainforests, or environmental groups that specialize in saving habitats. (See *Useful Addresses*.)
- Write to local governments, newspapers, politicians, and join local action groups, if important local habitats are threatened.
- Help green the world's cities: plant trees in urban areas, or start a nature reserve on derelict land. In Britain, help to plant the new 'Community Forests'.
- Garden organically. Create habitats by planting trees and wild flowers.
- Avoid reef souvenirs on holiday, since their collection is a major cause of destruction.

10
Inland Pollution

INTRODUCTION

In 1984, the Indian town of Bhopal experienced the worst ever industrial pollution accident, when an invisible cloud of toxic gas from a nearby factory smothered 40 sq km, killing as many as 5–10,000 and injuring 200,000![1] The parent company, Union Carbide, was operating under conditions unacceptable in the US.

On a less dramatic scale, we are steadily poisoning our planet with hundreds of millions of tons of potentially hazardous chemicals each year, spewing waste from industry, spraying whole continents with agro-chemicals, dumping sewage at sea, spilling oil from tankers. Persistent chemicals do not magically disappear . . .

CAUSES AND EFFECTS

Agriculture

In the US, the massive use of fertilizers and pesticides (fungicides, insecticides, herbicides) causes over $\frac{1}{2}$ of water pollution.[2] In Britain, after 25 years of improvement, river quality has declined steadily since 1979, with 1,000 miles now seriously polluted and the clean-up bill (to EEC standards) estimated at £6 billion; farming is largely responsible, with 56% of prosecutions in 1986 for pollution from agriculture, 42% from industry.[3]

Pesticides □ US usage almost tripled between 1965 and 1985.[4] 99% of all crops in Britain are sprayed at least once,[5] with 25% of pesticides not reviewed for safety for over 20 years[6] and none tested for long-term toxicity. This is the norm in the developed world. In the Third World, although neither so widely nor intensively used, usage is growing rapidly (India's production multiplied nearly 30-fold from 1960 to 1980, to 40,680 tons).[7] 25% of pesticides imported from the US were severely restricted or banned at home – only to return in imported food![2]

Wholesale pollution □ Pesticides kill off sensitive wildlife on farmland all over the world. In the Paris Basin they have caused a 70% reduction in 800 resident animal species.[8] And as far away as the Antarctic, Adelie penguins show detectable levels of DDT.

Drinking water □ Pesticides get into drinking-water supplies, with about 300 in Britain – and that's probably optimistic – containing levels above the legal EEC limit.[9] In the US, over 50 pesticides contaminate groundwater in at least 30 states, with more than $\frac{1}{4}$ of Iowans drinking contaminated water.

Food residues □ US residues could lead to a risk of 20,000 additional cancers each year.[4] UN Maximum Residue Levels (MRLs) in food are regularly exceeded in the UK. In a 1982–85 Ministry of Agriculture (MAFF) report, 28% of 648 samples of UK-produced vegetables (52% for imported food) contained residues above limits.[10] Up to 64% of pesticides applied to wheat may end up unaltered in bread.[5]

Direct poisonings □ Each year, between 400,000 and 2 million poisonings occur worldwide, mostly in the Third World, with about 10–40,000 deaths. In 1977, the fumigant DBCP was proved to cause sterility in 35 male chemical workers in California, but producers still allowed its use in Central America.[11]

Cancer □ 49 pesticides permitted for regular use in Britain have been linked with cancer; 90 with allergies or skin irritation; 61 with mutagenic effects (producing mutations); and 32 with birth defects.[12] None of the cocktails of chemicals has ever been tested. A British study showed that rates of birth defects in agricultural workers' children was above average.[5] And in the US, scientists reported a 6-fold increase in the risks of a cancer of the lymphatic system among Kansas farmers using certain herbicides for 20 days or more per year.[4]

Nitrates □ The world's fertilizer usage increased 10-fold from 1950 to 1989. In the US, 5-fold from 1950 to 1981, but it has fallen a little since.[7] And in Britain, 8-fold (for nitrogen) since the mid-1940s.[12]

Drinking water □ In Britain, 5 million receive tap water breaching the EEC nitrate limits. The Yorkshire Water Authority had to deliver bottled water to some areas to protect babies until a new supply was tapped.[3]

Health effects □ Nitrates have been linked with cancer of the stomach, and the Blue Baby Syndrome in newly borns.

Eutrophication □ When nitrates and phosphates get into waterways, from fields and sewage works, they stimulate algae growth, turning clear water into 'pea soup'. Plants are shaded out and virtually everything is suffocated if the algae population explodes.

Others □ Animal slurry, and the run-off from manure and silage, are very powerful pollutants, often leaching into waterways. Manure and slurry are often spread carelessly, polluting further.

Industry

Most countries have only a vague idea of their industrial pollution levels. In the US, the National Research Council estimates that no toxic effects information is available for 79% of the 48,500+ listed chemicals.[4] We could be in for some unpleasant surprises. Here is a grim sample of problems:

The developed world □ Manufactures 70,000 chemicals, with US industry spewing out at least 250 million tonnes of noxious waste each year, about 1 tonne per citizen, most landfilled or poured straight into waterways.[2] A probable 2.1 million tons of hazardous air pollutants were produced in 1987, including about 105,000 tons of carcinogens, which may be causing 2,000 cancer deaths each year and costing the US $40 billion in health care and lost productivity.[7] Carcinogens, including PCBs, are found in 99% of Americans, who, in 1982, had a 31% chance of contracting cancer before the age of 74; many of the sources were environmental.[2] Over 200 substances were found in the nation's groundwater (a source of drinking water), 37 were carcinogens and many had never been tested.[4] Greenpeace found over 800 synthetic chemicals in the Great Lakes, with up to 50% of some species of wildlife in some areas having visible defects.[13]

In Sweden, the pulping industry discharges 300,000 tonnes of highly polluting organochlorines each year (including tiny amounts of TCDD – the most toxic substance ever produced)[14] simply to provide bleached paper, whose necessity is almost entirely cosmetic. In Wales, after a century of coal burning, the Lower Swansea Valley is almost devoid of vegetation.[4]

Problem waste disposal sites□In West Germany, as many as 35,000 exist. And in the US, cleaning up old toxic waste sites will cost $23–100 billion.[4] In 1978, the Love Canal community in New York, built on top of a site used from the late 1940s to dump dioxin, lindane and mirex, was abandoned due to an unusual number of cancers and birth defects; the chemicals had taken just 30 years to surface.

Toxic waste trade□This has exploded in recent years, with dealers avoiding rising costs by dumping in poorer nations. Imports into Britain, where it is cheap and poorly monitored, increased 10-fold to 200,000 tonnes per year, 130,000 tonnes landfilled without treatment![15]

The Eastern Bloc□The USSR discharges 150 cu km (the equivalent of a lake 5x10 km in area and 3 km deep!) of polluted water into its waterways each year.[16] And Eastern Europe suffers the worst pollution on earth. In Poland, $\frac{1}{4}$ of the soil is unfit to grow food,[4] $\frac{1}{3}$ of rivers unfit for any use,[17] and less than 1% of water safe to drink, with (40–60 year old) male life expectancy back to 1952 levels and at least 1 in 3 expected to suffer an environmentally-induced illness.[4]

The Third World□Third World countries are increasingly producers of atmospheric pollution due to industrialization, with many developed-world industries setting up to take advantage of less stringent, often non-existent, regulations. Cities like Bombay, Beijing, and Mexico are amongst the most polluted in the world. Water pollution is a growing problem, with 70% of India's surface-water polluted, and 54 out of 78 rivers monitored in China seriously polluted with untreated sewage and industrial waste.[12] In Brazil, where pollution along the southern coast is horrendous, the industrial city of Cubatao is known as the 'Valley of Death'. Just to survive, children have to breathe medicated air in the local clinic every day.

Motor vehicles

One of the worst polluters in industrial nations.[3] In the UK, road vehicles account for 80% of lead emissions, 85% of carbon monoxide, 45% of nitrogen oxides, 28% of hydrocarbons, 16% of carbon dioxide,[18] and about 80% of London's black smoke.[19] Each car produces 250 kg of pollution per year. (See *The Transport Problem*.)

Sewage plants

In England and Wales, over 20% of main sewage plants broke the law in 1987, due to inadequate maintenance and investment.[11] They emit most of the phosphates in British water.[19]

WHAT HAS BEEN DONE

Agriculture

- Integrated Pest Management (IPM) – which uses 33–90% fewer pesticides than conventional farming – was being used on about 8% of US cropland in 1984. China probably has the best record, Brazil is using it, and Indonesia essentially made it national policy in 1986. Furthermore, Sweden and Denmark aim to halve pesticide use by 1992 and 1997 respectively. Some Third World governments, however, still subsidize pesticides between 19 and 89% of their cost.[4]
- In 1985, the 'Dirty Dozen' pesticides – 18 very dangerous chemical – were to be phased out globally and are already banned or severely restricted in at least 60 countries.
- In 1989, the EC drafted a directive for blanket controls on chemical fertilizers and manure, where nitrates reached more than 50 mg per litre in drinking-water sources.

Industry

- Virtually no country has a long-term strategy for safe industrial waste disposal; and few developing countries even have regulations. South Korea is one exception. Globally, Denmark and West Germany have the best records; all industries in Denmark and Bavaria must send waste to management companies.

- Better still, numerous companies (although few compared to the total) have reduced wastes: the Minnesota Mining and Manufacturing (3M) Company has halved wastes and saved nearly $300 million since 1975. The key was reusing wastes, changing manufacturing processes, and using different raw materials and safer products.[4]
- The June 1989 revisions to the US 1970 Clean Air Act aimed to remove an ambitious 75% of airborne toxic chemical emissions by 1995 and eliminate them shortly afterwards.
- In March 1989, in Basle, the first international toxic waste trade treaty was adopted (agreed in principle) by over 100 countries and signed (agreed and signed) by 34.
- In Britain, phosphate-free detergents, by Ecover, Clear Spring, and Ark, hold 5% of today's market.[16]

Cars

(See *The Transport Problem*.)

WHAT SHOULD BE DONE

Industry

- Pesticide use could be cut 50% over the next decade[4] and industrial waste by 50% in the next few years. (If we have the technology to put man on the Moon and send space ships past Pluto, this shouldn't be too taxing, surely?) This means tough legislation and fines, financial incentives, and powerful watchdogs. Cleaning up the air in the Los Angeles area would save $9.4 billion a year in health care, more than 3xs the cost of the clean-up![7]
- Establish an international fund to enforce the reduction of global pollution.
- Ban the hazardous waste trade.
- Introduce huge fines for polluters so polluting doesn't pay.

Agriculture

- Start on the road to a world organic farming system, using IPM as an intermediate step. (See *Agriculture*.)
- Suspend pesticides not tested to modern standards. Establish

strict pesticide levels in the environment, and designate water-protection zones where they are controlled to avoid water contamination (ditto for nitrates). Levy a sales tax (about 10%)[9] to cover monitoring and treatment costs.
- Move towards a nitrogen quota Europe-wide, and ensure all drinking water complies with EEC legal limits.

Sewage plants
- Improve plants everywhere so they are non-polluting: there is no need to turn an asset into a pollutant.

WHAT YOU CAN DO

We will get better pollution control laws only if enough people make a fuss about it.
- Report local pollution incidents to local water authorities, councils, newspapers, and Friends of the Earth. Write to the owners of local polluting factories.
- Write to your local politician demanding tighter controls on pesticide use. Put pressure on local governments not to use pesticides in public places.
- Write to your water authority about nitrate levels in your water. Inform your local paper, and ask them to print an article based on the Friends of the Earth factsheet. (See *Useful Addresses*.)
- Use environmentally-friendly household cleaners (in Britain: Ecover, Clear Spring, Ark, Tesco's own brand). Phosphates cause eutrophication (rapid growth of organic matter, too much creates damaging effects) in sweet and salt water all over Europe: 40% in Britain[20] originating from the 500,000 tons of household detergents used each year.[16]
- Garden organically; and compost leaves – burning them pollutes. Take rubber, plastics, old furniture to the tip as burning emits a lot of toxic fumes.

11
Ocean Pollution

INTRODUCTION

San Francisco Bay contains a deadly mass that includes cobalt, nickel, cadmium, and mercury, and it is getting worse[1] . . . The North Sea shows signs of collapsing as a viable ecosystem . . . The Mediterranean is the filthiest sea in the world, receiving an estimated 430 billion tonnes of pollution each year;[2] $\frac{1}{4}$ of its beaches are dangerously filthy and nearly all oysters and mussels are unsafe as food, with typhoid, paratyphoid, dysentery, polio, viral hepatitis, and food poisoning endemic[3] . . . The coastal waters of nearly every major Third World port are polluted with industrial waste and raw sewage, and it is getting worse . . . The Irish Sea is the world's most radioactive thanks to Sellafield[4] . . . And the Mersey river and its tributaries are probably the most polluted in Western Europe.[5]

We spew and dump growing amounts of waste into the oceans, with no idea how much they can absorb; yet they supply us with millions of tonnes of fish, support huge amounts of wildlife, have major effects on rainfall and climate, and are the backbone of the sulphur and sodium cycles. Yet again, man is playing Russian roulette with nature.

CAUSES

85% of ocean pollution comes from human activities on land, and 90% remains in coastal waters, the ocean's most productive areas.[6]

Industry
Discharge □ British rivers spew over 600,000 tonnes of cadmium, mercury, PCBs, lindane, and DDT into the North Sea each year.[7]

Dumping□2 million tonnes of noxious industrial waste are dumped into the Irish Sea,[8] and more than 3.5 million tonnes into the North Sea each year.[9]

Dredging□Contaminated dredging-spoil from harbours, containing nearly 13.3 million tonnes of heavy metals and chlorinated compounds, are dumped each year into the seas around Britain.

Ocean incineration□Ocean incineration is banned in the Mediterranean, the Baltic, and the waters off the US. It is allowed only in the North Sea, and although due to be phased out, the zone off Scarborough burns up to 100,000 tonnes of hazardous wastes each year,[7] with pollutants likely to enter the sea afterwards.

Air pollution□Acid rain, plus other air pollution, is a major form of ocean pollution. (See *Acid Rain.*)

Agriculture

Waters off the French Mediterranean coast receive 115,000 tonnes of phosphates and 340,000 tonnes of nitrates each year, mainly from agricultural run-off.[2] (See *Inland Pollution.*)

Nuclear power stations

The UK coast is dotted with nuclear plants discharging radioactivity. Millions of gallons of radioactive effluent discharge daily into the Irish Sea, with up to $\frac{1}{2}$ tonne of plutonium (enough to kill 500 million in theory[10]) already there.[11] There's also the risk of accidental release. (See *Nuclear Power.*)

Sewage

The discharge of un- or partially-treated sewage into the sea creates considerable pollution around New York, San Francisco, Sydney, Athens, Barcelona, Venice, and Marseilles. 50 million around the Mediterranean deposit almost 85% of their sewage into the sea untreated.[3] 12 million do the same in Britain in the summer,[9] with a further 6 million tonnes of sewage sludge dumped in the North Sea each year;[7] both contain heavy metals and other industrial waste.

Oil

Marine-oil pollution is about 3.5 million tonnes per year, 48% from land[10] – the rest from ships, much deliberate. On Good Friday 1989, the Exxon Valdez supertanker produced the biggest oil spill in US history, smothering over 4,800 sq km of the ecologically sensitive Prince William Sound off southern Alaska[12] with 11 million gallons of crude oil.[7] The clean-up response was slow and inadequate. The official body-count to mid September 1989 was 34,434 sea birds, 9,994 sea otters, 147 bald eagles, and up to 16 whales.[12] The birds retrieved are believed to represent only 10–30% of the kill, bringing numbers up to 100–300,000, unprecedented in oil spill history.[13]

EFFECTS

Algae blooms

Blooms of algae (fed by nutrients from fertilizers, sewage, and domestic detergents) have used up the oxygen over huge areas of ocean, killing fish, molluscs, and crustaceans. These Dead Zones are afloat in the Gulf of Mexico, the Adriatic, and the Baltic, with others proliferating worldwide.

Hazards of rubbish

Every day, masses of plastic debris are poured into the sea. Endangered turtles are killed by eating plastic bags resembling jellyfish. In the North Pacific, an estimated 50,000 fur seals are drowned each year in thousands of miles of lost, floating synthetic nets.

Beaches

Nearly 200 out of 690 British beaches are likely to be affected by untreated sewage;[14] less than 50% reach mandatory standards. Using Canada's tighter controls, over 90% would be closed as health hazards.[15]

Fish stocks

Numerous estuaries – spawning and breeding grounds of many fish and shellfish – are dying, and the remaining sedentary animals, particularly shellfish, are terribly contaminated. 33% of US shellfish beds were closed due to pollution in 1987.[10] And surveys around the Thames Estuary found 11% of fish had cancerous tumours or bacterial skin diseases, although Greenpeace suggested that in areas this rose to 34%.[13]

Human health

In the New York Bight, one of the most polluted of US coasts, dangerous levels of faecal bacteria, which cause numerous diseases, were found in mussels.[3] In North Devon, Britain, people were warned to eat not more than 1lb of shrimps or 4oz of shellfish to stay within WHO cadmium limits.[7] And according to a report from 20 of the world's leading marine biologists, sewage contamination of sea water causes many human diseases including cholera and hepatitis; what's more, the Aids virus survives in sewage-polluted seas for more than $1\frac{1}{2}$ days![16]

Wildlife

In 1987 and 1988, 100s of dead dolphins were found on beaches from Maine to Florida. In Massachusetts, 14 dead humpback whales were washed ashore in a few days in 1988. And in the Gulf of Maine, common seals have the highest pesticide levels of any US mammal.[1]

North Sea seal virus □ Signs of the North Sea collapsing as a viable ecosystem have appeared relatively quickly, being one of the most serious recent environmental disasters. In 1988, a viral epidemic, believed to be a form of canine distemper, killed 15,000 (or 50%) of common seals in the North Sea[17] and a total of 17,500 seals in Europe.[18] Central to the disaster were overfishing, ocean pollution (one dead baby seal contained over 1,000 contaminants),[17] overfertilization (eutrophication), and acid rain. In addition, there have been horrific algae blooms and massive sea-bird breeding failures.

WHAT HAS BEEN DONE

About 100,000 chemicals are present in the North Sea, many highly poisonous; yet the British Ministry of Agriculture,

Fisheries, and Food monitors only 15 routinely.[19] Such neglect is the global norm.

- In Canada, the US, and Japan, 75% of sewage plants have secondary treatment before sea discharge. In Sweden, 80% have tertiary treatment.[10]
- Oil released at sea has been considerably reduced by additives (which allow the culprits to be fingerprinted), and by the International Convention for the Prevention of Pollution from ships (MARPOL).
- UNEP (United Nations Environmental Programme) established its Regional Seas programme in 1974, supported by 120 nations. The Mediterranean Plan, uniting the 17 nations in a clean-up, was the pilot scheme. But much still needs to be done.
- In 1985, a moratorium on sea dumping of radioactive waste was called for.
- During 1985, the 13 states of the South Pacific Forum voted to create a nuclear-free zone, to stop dumping and weapons testing.
- The November 1987 North Sea Conference agreed to: reduce persistent toxics to rivers and estuaries by 50%; end the dumping of harmful wastes by the end of 1989; reduce the input of nutrients and radioactivity; prohibit the dumping of garbage from ships; and terminate ocean incineration by 1994. Only Britain insisted on continuing to dump sewage sludge.
- The British government is being taken to the European Court over its failure to meet the 1985 deadline for minimum quality standards for beaches.

WHAT SHOULD BE DONE

- Develop industrial waste reduction, to reduce pollution at source. (See *Inland Pollution*.)
- Reduce toxic discharges into rivers and seas by 50% by 1995 in the West, and as soon as feasible in the Third World.
- Ban ocean dumping as soon as possible. It is criminal that sewage, instead of being a million dollar asset (fertilizer, soil improver, building material) is a million dollar pollution problem.

61

- Ban all radioactive discharges into the oceans.
- Introduce massive fines and clean-up costs to make the oil giants toughen up on safety.
- Ban ocean incineration globally to prevent it starting elsewhere. As long as industry can rely on it, alternatives will not be developed.

WHAT YOU CAN DO

- For local problems, get your local authority to test for bacteria, and ask your water authority if it controls industrial effluent at its sea outfalls.
- Report details of birds killed by oil – in Britain, to the RSPB or BTO. Send bird rings to the British Natural History Museum or the RSPB. (See *Useful Addresses*.)
- Watch out for oil drums, packages marked 'Hazard', fishing nets, packing cases. In Britain, the Advisory Committee on Pollution of the Sea (see *Useful Addresses*) keeps a register and would value information on whereabouts. With hazard or radioactive signs, contact the coastguard or police immediately.
- Join environmental groups fighting for the oceans. In Britain: Greenpeace, WWF, Friends of the Earth, or the Marine Conservation Society.

12
The Transport Problem

INTRODUCTION

Observing us from space, aliens might well be puzzled why we devote so much time and energy to the four-wheeled metal boxes that wreak havoc wherever they go.

In the countryside, roads carve up ever increasing areas of land, destroying valuable habitats and shattering the peace and quiet. In the city, roads are jam-packed and dangerous, public transport is overcrowded and slow, and residential streets are polluted and noisy. Traffic controls us; we should control it.

CAUSES

The heart of the problem is overemphasis on the car and underemphasis on public transport.

The car

The car is noisy, highly polluting, dangerous, and energy-intensive; and useful as it is, collective disadvantages often outweigh individual advantages. Motor vehicle numbers are growing daily, with 500 million globally in 1988,[1] about 400 million of them cars.[2] Over 22 million of these were in Britain,[3] where road traffic increased by 27% from 1984 to 1989 and is predicted to rise a further 83–142% by 2025.[4] By 1985, 9 out of 10 passenger km travelled in Britain were by road,[1] due to the convenience of the car (mainly); the move towards fewer, bigger shopping centres, schools, hospitals; the fact that so many people use them to commute to work; and the government's transport policy.

Lorries

These are noisy, and cause immense damage to roads, bridges, houses. Furthermore, diesel lorries cause up to 10xs more pollution than other transport.[5] In Britain, the shift of freight from rail to road has increased the decline of rail and the congestion of roads.

Poor public transport

Per passenger, van pools, public cars, buses, and rail use $\frac{1}{4}$ of the fuel that private cars or planes use. And, per ton of freight, trains and ships use less than $\frac{1}{3}$ of the fuel that trucks would need.[6] But in Britain, in the last three decades, 40% of the railways have been closed, 29% of bus services cut,[7] and still the government wants to destroy what's left, despite 40% of households being without a car. Similarly in the US, the taxpayer spent $80 billion on highways and only $6 billion on railways during the 1980s, with public transport accounting for only 3% of inter-city transport, even though rail is purpose-built for the long distances.[8] Meanwhile, most other Western nations are investing heavily in railways, trams, subways, etc. In Europe, on average, 0.67% of GDP is invested in rail, in Britain 0.23%.[9]

Government policies

Britain has the model Environmentally-Unfriendly transport policy. It favours the road lobby and the car. Cyclists and pedestrians are largely ignored. Public transport is run down, and is consequently dirty, unreliable, overcrowded. Britain's rail fares are the most expensive in Europe,[10] and the roads some of the most congested.[11] Rail has tighter financial constraints in Britain than in any other industrial nation; company cars are subsidized more than anywhere in Europe, and the bus regulation is comparable only in Chile, Kuala Lumpur, and Jamaica.[8]

EFFECTS

Congestion

Cars block city roads, take up massive amounts of space and yet usually contain only 1 or 2 travellers. In Britain, even the road industry estimates urban congestion costs at £8 billion per year.[7] Furthermore, new roads – including urban motorways – often encourage more traffic and congestion.

Noise

Noise is very stressful, and is an unfortunate fact of life for many urban-dwellers. In the country, large roads destroy the peace with their continual hum.

Disruption

New roads can tear local communities apart, slicing through residential areas, cutting off homes from shops, schools, workplaces.

Employment

In terms of local communities, new roads usually destroy more jobs than they create.

Urban sprawl

Further road construction encourages urban sprawl.

Accidents

In the US, about 50,000 a year die on the roads;[12] in Britain 6,000 (400 are children,[13] representing 15% of child deaths), with nearly 300,000 injured.[14] Apart from the terrible heartache, this costs Britain £2.8 billion per year.[13]

Pollution

Motor vehicles are one of the worst polluters in industrial nations,[1] producing over 1,000 chemicals,[15] and in Britain, account for 80% of lead emissions, 85% of carbon monoxide, 45% of nitrous oxides, 28% of hydrocarbons, 16% of carbon dioxide,[16] and about 80% of London's black smoke.[12]

Nitrous oxides cause smogs and acid rain. Hydrocarbons are largely responsible for smogs that used to choke cities like Tokyo and Los Angeles (LA), and which are now appearing in cities like Ankara and Mexico City. Ozone causes smogs, crop damage, and is highly poisonous. Lead is highly toxic, damaging brain and nervous systems, particularly in children and pregnant women; heavily leaded petrols are the norm in the Third World. Even fumes (including unleaded) from petrol pumps and stations are damaging.

Health hazards

Car emissions contain about 30 carcinogens. Diesel is worse. 12% of US lung cancer deaths are caused by motor vehicle emissions; in Britain, this could mean 3–4,000 deaths each year.[12] Health damage from car pollution costs Sweden £40–170 million each year.

Acid rain

30% of British acid rain comes from nitrous oxides, of which 40% is from traffic.[17] Thus, traffic is responsible for 12% of British acid rain. (See *Acid Rain*.)

The Greenhouse Effect

30% of carbon dioxide comes from the transport sector in the US[18] and France[19], and 20% in Britain (96% from road transport). Thus, in Britain, to reach a 20% cut in carbon dioxide by 2005, without cutting back on road transport, will require a 50% cut in all other sources.[4] (See *The Greenhouse Effect*.)

Wildlife

Britain has lost nearly 200 sq km – that's an area 6 by 12 miles – under 1,847 miles of motorway.[1] And at least 110 Sites of Special Scientific Interest (SSSIs – some of Britain's best habitats) have recently been destroyed or damaged, or are threatened, by new roads.[8]

Loss of agricultural land

Paving more and more land with roads and parking spaces means cars compete with farmers.[2]

Energy consumption

Transport is the largest, most rapidly growing drain on world oil reserves,[6] with road transport alone consuming $\frac{1}{3}$ of world oil,[20] and transport in general consuming 63% in the US[6] and over 60% in Britain.[21] Furthermore, cars take the energy equivalent of 335 gallons of oil to manufacture, producing much pollution in the process.[1] (See *Overconsumption*.)

Loss of crop yields

Ozone pollution in the 1980s led to estimated crop yield losses of 5%, perhaps 10%, in the US.

Other

In the US, the hidden price of the car, for road building and maintenance, police and fire services, etc. is about $300 billion a year, paid for by car and non-car owners alike.[2]

WHAT HAS BEEN DONE

Some things are being done to alleviate the symptoms, but little to tackle the causes.

Alleviating the symptoms

Unleaded petrol □ Leaded petrol has been banned in countries like the US and Japan, and in many European nations unleaded sales are high – almost 60% of sales in West Germany.[22] In Britain, after a long uphill struggle, it is at last widely available, accounting for 29% of total petrol pump consumption by mid-1990[23] with all new cars required to be able to use it by the end of 1990. Lead, however, is only one of many pollutants, so this is but a small step in the right direction.

Catalytic converters □ Three-way catalysts are the most advanced technology for decreasing vehicle pollution, converting hydrocarbons and carbon monoxide to water and carbon dioxide, and nitrous oxides to nitrogen. They impair neither performance nor fuel efficiency. $\frac{1}{3}$–$\frac{1}{2}$ of cars globally have cats. In the US, they have been law for all new cars since 1975, leading to a reduction of 62% for nitrous oxides and 85 and 87% for carbon monoxide and hydrocarbons over the life of the vehicle![2] Canada, Japan, and Australia have followed suit. Denmark, Mexico, Taiwan, South Korea, and Brazil intend to do likewise. Catalysts are mandatory in Sweden, Norway, Switzerland, and Austria. But in Britain, of course, only a few makes of car had cats at the end of 1989. In June 1989, however, the EC finally adopted tough US emission standards for all new cars from the end of 1992, meaning cats will have to be fitted.

General pollution □ June 1989 revisions to the US 1970 Clean Air Act include a target of 500,000 methanol vehicles sold per year by 1995 and 1 million after 1997. To combat LA smog, southern Californian authorities have banned petrol and diesel vehicles by 2007. Employers not organizing car share schemes are heavily penalized. And nitrogen oxide and hydrocarbons will be reduced up to 60% by 1996; with further cuts planned for 2003.

The Dutch voted in February 1989 to grant tax breaks on low pollution cars.

Fuel efficiency □ Between 1972 and 1982, cars increased by $\frac{1}{3}$, but fuel consumed in leading car producing nations fell 4%, due to better fuel economy.[1] In the US (although efficiency doesn't reach European or Japanese standards, where they are testing cars close to 100 mpg) cars have nearly doubled in economy since 1973.[6] In France, they are seriously considering banning the manufacture of large cars.

Traffic calming □ In Germany, Scandinavia, and Holland, large-scale pedestrianization and traffic calming (the use of speed humps, width restrictions, street furniture, and parking control) enhance towns.

Car bans □ In Athens, Berlin, Hamburg, and Munich, cars are being severely restricted in the city centres.

Lorries □ Many countries ban lorries in towns on weekends and public holidays. Switzerland has the lowest lorry weights in Europe at 28 tonnes.

Noise □ Austria has banned lorries driving at night, to combat noise.

Tackling the causes

Public transport □ In Europe, fast, clean, efficient public transport manages to get people out of their cars, benefits all, and protects the environment. Rail is the only way of moving millions in and out of cities with minimal impact – Europeans have accepted this for decades, the Japanese too (in Tokyo, only 15% of commuters drive to work),[2] even the Americans are following suit. Some countries tax cars entering cities, using the revenue to finance alternatives like park and ride schemes. In Switzerland, public transport is cheap, expanding, and heavily subsidized; cycling is encouraged. And even in Britain, when the Greater London Council (GLC) introduced a cheaper, better service in the 1980s, bus use rose 13%, tube 44%, and car commuting fell 21%.

Bicycles □ The most energy-efficient transport invented, there are 800 million globally, with 3xs as many produced each year as cars. In the Third World, they are important in national economies, especially in Asia; unfortunately, Africa and Latin America lag behind. India is now a major world producer, with 90% of exports going to developing countries. In Bangladesh, trishaws transport more tonnage than all motor vehicles! In the West, Holland, Denmark, and West Germany have the best record. The Dutch National Environmental Policy Plan will encourage bikes for journeys of 5–10 km; for longer journeys, trains – not cars or planes. In Japan, in 1980, 15% of commuters rode bikes to work or to the station.

New technologies

Hydrogen, generated by solar electricity in desert plants, could provide the fuel of the future, emitting no carbon dioxide or sulphur dioxides (just a little nitrous oxide), and as cheap as methanol or ethanol.[9]

WHAT SHOULD BE DONE

Short-term: improve public transport, increase fuel efficiency, decrease pollution. Long-term: plan developments to reduce transport needs – and make the smaller number of cars non-polluting. Computerized shopping delivery services and working at home by computer may become common.[2]

- Double fuel economy of cars and light trucks by 2000.
- In Europe, introduce US diesel emission laws; and advance the date for the compulsory fitting of cats.
- Remove pro-car and -lorry taxes; introduce tax incentives on fuel efficient cars; increase petrol taxes.
- Reduce speed limits; give priority to pedestrians and cyclists in residential streets; pedestrianize large areas of all city

centres; ban lorries from towns on weekends and holidays.
- Make public transport cheap, reliable, and efficient. Shift freight from road to rail. Encourage bike use on short journeys (cold engines cause the most pollution): many commuters come into this category.

Pleasant cities will encourage business investment and people to live there, reducing development of the countryside.

WHAT YOU CAN DO

- Walk, cycle, or take public transport wherever possible. Make only essential journeys. Shop locally. Share your car to work or taking the kids to school: a car shared is pollution halved. Lobby public transport operators to raise standards. Join bus users' groups and cycle campaign groups.
- Buy small cars, drive slowly, keep them well-tuned, use unleaded, get a cat fitted (if possible). Don't rush to diesel, which produces more carcinogens.
- Reclaim your own street: traffic wardens will deal with illegal parking, police with speeding. In residential streets, consider road humps, street furniture, width restrictions.[14]
- In Britain, write to your local MP, and MPs for transport, protesting against the White Paper 'Roads to Prosperity', which proposes to increase public spending on roads from £5 billion to more than £12 billion.

13
Nuclear Power

INTRODUCTION

Nuclear power was developed out of the military programme in the 1950s, with the first reactor constructed in 1942 in Chicago, producing 200 watts of heat. The world's first commercial station was built in 1956 at Calder Hall in Britain, although its main role was to produce plutonium for nuclear bombs, not cheap electricity.

By 1988, 417 reactors[1] in 26 countries[2] supplied 17% of world electricity[1] and 2% of energy.[3] 80% was produced by 8 countries, with France – and its love affair for nuclear power – at the top of the list supplying 69.8% of electricity, then 50.3% in Sweden, 29.4% in West Germany, 24.7% in Japan, 18.4% in Britain, 16.6% in the US, 14.7% in Canada, and 10% in the USSR.[2]

THE PROBLEMS

In the 1950s, nuclear power was billed as a technical dream, a miraculous source of energy 'too cheap to meter'; now, it is environmentally and economically too nightmarish to contemplate. Consequently, the last 10 years have seen orders for new plants slowing to a trickle. Some of the stings in the tail include:

Technical and financial difficulties

Every reactor type in Britain has had problems, despite a colossal £16.3 billion spent on Research and Development (R&D) since 1958.[4]

- In stations over 1,000 megawatts, the average efficiency is 58% compared to an 80% design rating.
- Electricity is more expensive than from coal-fired stations – up to 50% more with Magnox stations.[3]
- Construction delays and huge financial over-runs are

71

typical, with US plants costing 5–10xs more than projected,[5] and Sizewell B, in Britain, quoted at £1.2 billion at the inquiry (the equivalent of more than 50 new general hospitals!)[6], unlikely to cost less than £2 billion.

- British Pressurized Water Reactors (PWRs) give worker radioactivity 25–500% higher than the industry's target.[7]
- In the US, estimated decommissioning costs (disassembling and cleaning up retired reactors) range between £200 and £700 million.[2] In Britain, decommissioning the Berkeley and Magnox reactors will take 120–150 years and cost about the same.[8]
- Insuring against potential claims from a serious accident is very expensive.

Radioactive waste and pollution

- Uranium mining (85% mined outside Eastern Europe comes from North America, Southern Africa, and Australia)[2] produces 100,000 tonnes of radioactive tailings and 3.5 million litres of liquid,[3] (which emit radioactive radon gas for over 500,000 years),[9] for every 1,000 tonnes of fuel produced.[3]
- After more than 30 years, a *safe* disposal method for radioactive waste has still not been found, although some is still highly dangerous after 250,000 years (50,000 years ago man had just learned to use fire!).[3] In the US, 12,000 tonnes of high-level waste is already in storage – this is expected to quadruple in the next 15 years – and must be kept away from living creatures, including humans, for 10,000 years.[2]
- 2 million gallons of radioactive effluent are discharged into the Irish Sea daily.[3] Up to $\frac{1}{2}$ tonne of plutonium is already there.[10] (See *Ocean Pollution*.)
- Clean-up costs from the US nuclear weapons programme were more than $40 billion by December 1988.[2]

Effects on human health

- Around Sellafield, house dust contains plutonium levels up to 6,000xs higher than elsewhere,[3] and radioactive contamination in general exceeds official safety limits by nearly 5xs.[11] Leukaemia levels are 10xs the national average.[3]

- The US National Research Council found the cancer risk from low doses of radiation (from X- and gamma rays) to be 3–4xs higher than previously thought, with no totally safe level.[12] At present, radiation limits for the general public are 5.0 millisieverts in the UK, whilst it is a tiny 0.35 in West Germany, and 0.25 in the US.

Nuclear weapons production

The power industry is closely linked to bomb manufacture, which uses similar technologies. In the US, though, there has been no reprocessing (the method of getting bomb-making materials from power station waste) of civil nuclear fuel since 1971, due to the dangers of proliferation.

Nuclear weapons proliferation

Some non-nuclear weapons states, which possess nuclear power, have started to make weapons (India, Pakistan, South Africa, Israel, Iraq). The Nuclear Non-Proliferation Treaty – designed to limit the bomb to the 5 nations currently possessing them – has been undermined by Britain, West Germany, and the US who have sold technology and expertise to non-signatories of the Treaty. (See *The Arms Race*.)

Nuclear weapons accidents

From 10 accidents, the US and Soviet navies have lost about 50 nuclear weapons and 9 nuclear reactors on the ocean floor.[1]

Reactor accidents

The most serious risk. Worldwide, there have been 2 major accidents (see below) and countless minor ones during 3,000 'reactor years'. At this rate, we can expect a serious accident every 4 years.[7] The Chief Inspector for Nuclear Safety at Electricité de France admits there is a 'several per cent' chance of a serious accident occurring in France within the next 20 years![13]

Three Mile Island□ In 1979, the Three Mile Island plant in

73

the US suffered partial melt-down, costing over $1 billion to clean up.[3]

Chernobyl □ In 1986, a reactor exploded at the Chernobyl plant in the USSR, producing more atmospheric radioactivity than all nuclear tests in history.[14] A contaminating radioactive cloud drifted quickly over most of Europe. About 135,000 were evacuated from a 100 km area,[7] with 30 killed immediately,[15] rising to 250.[16] The cancer rate is rising, and is set to cause as many as 100,000 deaths in the USSR over the next 40 years, and 500 as far away as Britain.[14] By 1990, the medical and ecological effects were very much greater than predicted, with perhaps up to 1 million children suffering severe effects (all children in the contaminated area have swollen thyroids) and perhaps another 3 million people needing to be evacuated. In the Ukraine alone, 5 million ha (an area $\frac{1}{5}$ the size of Britain) of farmland and 1.5 million ha of forest were contaminated.[17] The cost to the USSR reached an estimated £8 billion by 1988,[15] and more than £10 billion to the world.[18]

WHAT HAS BEEN DONE

After Chernobyl, nuclear development has slowed down, with countries everywhere turning to coal as an alternative. Due to public fears, Italy, Austria, and Switzerland have halted further development; Venezuela, Yugoslavia, and Israel have abandoned planned projects; and the USSR has halted construction on a number of reactors after massive demonstrations. Sweden, with 50.3% of electricity from nuclear fuel, held a referendum and decided to close all plants by 2010.

- In the 10 years after Three Mile Island, not one reactor was ordered in the US, but 100 were cancelled. Unfortunately, new moves from Washington, using the fallacious justification of curbing the GE, may give new life to the industry.
- In November 1989, Britain abandoned plans to build 3 new PWRs, as it withdrew the nuclear plants from the 1990 sale of the electricity industry, thus ending hopes of expanding nuclear power.

WHAT SHOULD BE DONE

Short-term: end all radioactive discharges into the sea, and in Britain, end feather-bedding for the industry. Within a decade, phase out all nuclear plants globally.[4]

- The billions of dollars saved should go into energy efficiency, renewables, combined heat and power schemes (CHP), and cleaner coal-fired stations. In the UK, this would create a *net additional* 250,000 long-term jobs over the next 15 years, compared to 20,000 lost.[19] (See *Energy*.)
- Through increased energy efficiency, in Britain, electricity demand could be cut by 70%, providing the same services, 5–10xs cheaper. Renewables could provide 20% of British energy by 2020.[7] Where, then, is the need for nuclear power? (See *Energy*.)

WHAT YOU CAN DO

- Avoid wasting electricity (for instance, running hot water taps unnecessarily): in Britain 17% of it comes from nuclear sources.
- When you pay your electricity bill, protest against the percentage contributing to nuclear supplies.
- Complain to your electricity company, your politician, the Secretary of State for Energy. Remember, politicians take note of letters.
- Make a big fuss, quickly, about any proposed dumps or nuclear plants in your community. Get the local and national press in.

14
Energy

INTRODUCTION

Our prolific use of energy in the developed world cannot be sustained. Each person uses the energy equivalent of 6 tonnes of coal a year[1] – mainly as electricity and fossil fuels. This is the main cause of some of our most critical problems. An environmental energy strategy is, therefore, imperative in order to reach a sustainable society.

Between 1973 (with the first oil price leap) and 1983, increased efficiency slowed consumption increases. Unfortunately, since 1986, when oil prices plunged, governments have been complacent, with funding for renewables dropping in many countries (just when we need it most). In 1988, energy consumption jumped again.

PROBLEMS

Greenhouse Effect

This is the world's foremost environmental problem, with fossil fuels (from electricity production, heating, and transport) the largest contributor, about 40% of the effect.[2] In Britain, power stations are the largest single contributor, 20% of the effect.[3] (See *The Greenhouse Effect*.)

Acid rain

British acid rain contains 70% sulphur dioxide, and about 30% nitrous oxides.[4] Power stations produce 70%[1] and 40%[4] respectively – thus responsible for 61% of acid rain. (See *Acid Rain*.)

Nuclear pollution

Some of today's radioactive waste will still be highly dangerous in 250,000 years![5] (See *Nuclear Power*.)

Oil pollution

About 3.5 million tonnes of oil pollute the world's oceans each year, with disastrous effects on wildlife.[6] (See *Ocean Pollution*.)

Habitat destruction

Hydro-electric power (HEP) floods whole valleys, slag heaps desecrate the landscape, electricity pylons criss-cross the countryside, and open-cast mining rips everything apart.

Resource depletion

Ironically, the consequences of fossil fuel pollution are now more likely to limit their use than are limited supplies. It is, however, worth noting that the world economy is powered by non-renewable fuels, with only 60 years of oil[7] and 50 of natural gas, 60 of uranium,[8] and 250 of coal left at present rates of consumption.[7]

SOLUTIONS

Short-term: greatly improve energy efficiency; long-term: turn to renewable energy.

Energy efficiency

Most developed countries have improved efficiency 20–30% since 1973, saving $250 billion worth of oil, coal, nuclear power annually. Japan, the most efficient nation, uses only 4% of GNP to pay its fuel bill; the US 10%, thus paying a $200 billion inefficiency tax, relatively speaking.[9] Eastern Europe and the USSR are rather inefficient – about $\frac{1}{2}$ that of Western Europe.[10] And most of the Third World is now increasing consumption, with efficiencies of about $\frac{1}{3}$ that of the rich countries,[11] except Taiwan, South Korea, and Brazil, which have started to invest in it.

Britain, using the best available technology, could reduce mean electricity demand by 70%, providing the same services 5–10xs cheaper, and saving a minimum of £7 billion in fuel bills per year by 1995.[12] In India, industrial efficiency could be improved 15–30%, by good housekeeping. But most significantly, energy efficiency gains of at least 50% are available in every sector of the world economy: the limiting factor is institutional.[13]

Heating□ Britain uses $\frac{1}{3}$ of its energy to heat buildings. Up to 40% could be saved by insulating, draught-proofing, fitting individual thermostats, cavity wall insulation, double glazing, and replacing old boilers.[8] Buildings can be constructed to use $\frac{1}{3}$–$\frac{1}{10}$ of the energy, with more than 20,000 super-insulated houses in North America,[13] requiring little heat from conventional heat sources.

Appliances□ 11.5% energy savings are available from the best lighting, refrigerator, and industrial motor technology.[3] Japanese household appliances use 50% less energy than in the mid-1970s.[7] The US 1987 National Appliance Act, which requires energy labelling, will save enough energy by 2000 to eliminate 10 large power stations, 342 million tons of carbon dioxide, and save $28 billion.[14]

Lighting□ Consumes about 20% of US electricity. The full application of technology offers some of the largest, most economical savings, with the potential of early retirement for 40 large US power plants. Swapping a 75 watt bulb with an (equally bright) 18 watt fluorescent bulb saves 180 kg of coal over its lifetime, and eliminates 130 kg of carbon dioxide.

Cars□ Increasing fuel efficiency of US cars from 13.1 to 17.9 mpg between 1973 and 1985 saved 20 billion gallons of petrol per year. Doubling the efficiency of European cars to 50 mpg would lower annual fuel bills almost $400, cut pollution, reduce carbon dioxide by 450 kg per year, and lower oil consumption.[13] Already most manufacturers have developed prototype 100 mpg cars.[8] (See *The Transport Problem*.)

Airlines□ Airlines have cut fuel per passenger km by almost $\frac{1}{3}$.[72]

Industry□ In Japan, the law requires companies with high-energy consumption to employ full-time energy managers.[13]

Developing world□ Improving cooking stove efficiency from 20% (as it is now) to 50% would cut wood demand by 50%, greatly reducing pressures on forests; this would cost governments only $10 to buy each stove.[7]

Renewable energy

An energy source is renewable if sustained use will not permanently deplete supplies, and includes wind, sunlight, running water, plants, forest products. Renewables are not as economic as energy efficiency, but costs are falling and reliability improving. And despite erratic political and financial support, these energy sources have made remarkable strides in the past decade, now providing 21% of global energy: 15% as biomass (although much as unsustainable fuelwood collection), 6% as hydropower. Brazil, Israel, Japan, the Philippines, and Sweden are well on the renewable path. India plans major increases by 2000. And Greece gives them strong political backing, with 63% of the energy R&D budget.[13]

Biomass □ Biomass is plant energy and includes forestry products, crop residues, animal wastes, and energy crops. Nearly 50% of world population (mostly in the Third World where fossil fuels and electricity are often absent in rural areas) rely on biomass, mostly as wood, and it is the main fuel for 80% of people in the Third World.[7] However, the potential for biomass is hardly tapped.

Possibilities in the Third World include: the fermentation of the sugar in sugar-cane, cassava, maize to ethanol; small wood-fired stations fuelled by quick-growing plantations; and the fermentation of animal dung, human excreta, or crop residues to methane (Bio-gas).

Possibilities in Britain (equivalent to 3 Sizewell B nuclear plants)[15] include: straw- and wood-fired boilers, methane from sewage and agricultural waste, refuse incineration, and biomass electricity from willow and poplar plantations – not to mention hedge and woodland coppicing (see below). Energy crops, however, should be grown on marginal, not good agricultural, land.[10]

Ethanol □ Brazil and the US have the 2 largest programmes. In Brazil, sugar-cane grown for fuel provided about 62% of the country's auto fuel in 1988,[10] slashing oil imports and creating about 475,000 full-time jobs. At least 12 other countries have programmes.[13] (It should, however, be noted that in Brazil the land occupied by sugar-cane for this purpose was previously used for food crops – and could still be used for that purpose.)

Hydroelectric power (HEP) □ Mega- and small dams generate 25% of world electricity and about 5% of energy.[7] China, Brazil, and India have the most ambitious projects, with some monster dams – Brazil's 12,600 megawatt Itaipu Dam is 5 miles long and 700 feet high. The Third World has the greatest potential, although huge dams have huge tradeoffs, including: serious effects on the ecology of the river and farmland downstream; increased earthquakes; expanded breeding grounds for diseases; vast destruction of virgin forest (and thus the homes of millions of tribal people); and that the foreign contractors and urban elites are the main beneficiaries, not the urban poor. Small-scale, decentralized dams are far more appropriate.

Solar □ The sun supplies more energy to the earth in an hour than man consumes in a year;[8] yet astoundingly we use precious little of this inexhaustible free energy supply. This should supply nearly all the world's domestic hot water in the future, and most of the electricity (with battery storage for night time) in hot countries, especially the Third World where it is often cheaper, quicker, and more reliable than expanding the electricity grid. In the US, this could supply an estimated 50%+ of electricity in 40–50 years.[10]

Cyprus, the largest user per capita, has solar water heaters on 90% of houses and numerous apartment buildings and hotels. In Israel, this is 65%; and in Japan and Australia, a significant percentage.[13]

Currently, however, Third World rural electrification relying on solar cells (as found in solar calculators) is very slow, with greatest progress in the Dominican Republic, French Polynesia, and Greece. It is used for refrigerating vaccines, pumping irrigation water, and lighting and entertainment facilities in homes.

Solar thermal power, which focuses sunlight on to oil-filled tubes, captures an amazing 22% of solar energy at $\frac{2}{3}$ the cost per kWh of nuclear power. Such plants could stretch across many deserts in the future, exporting electricity and producing hydrogen for cars.[10]

Wind □ There are more than 20,000 electricity-producing windmills[10] in 95 countries, with the international wind power generating market expanding 17-fold from 1981 to 1986. The US leads in intermediate-sized turbines,[13] with California aiming to get 10% of its electricity from wind farms by 2000.[8] The European market is increasing. India, Denmark, China, and the Netherlands have optimistic plans for the next 5–10 years – India's is the most ambitious, with a planned 5,000 megawatts by 2000.[13]

The world could get 10% of its electricity from wind by 2030; the US 10–20%,[10] Britain at least 20% (mainly from large wind farms, possibly offshore to decrease environmental impact).[8] Income from wind farms in the US Great Plains could dwarf farmers' current $30 per ha ranching incomes.[10] Costs will continue to decrease as demand increases.[13]

Geothermal □ Geothermal power (the Earth's temperature rises 1° Celsius every 30 metres down) has progressed dramatically in recent years,[13] with 130 plants[7] and 5,000 megawatts worldwide, more than half since 1980.[13] The US, the Philippines, Mexico, Italy, Japan are among the leading nations in this field; and Iceland and Indonesia have great potential. In Britain, 20% live in suitable areas, with a small project started in Southampton in 1986.[8]

Power from the sea □ There are 4 types: thermal energy conversion, and wave, tidal, and current power.
Wave power □ Britain has one of the best wave climates globally, and, with adequate funding, it could produce 20–30% of current electricity consumption in the near future, especially in remote islands.[8]
Tidal □ 6 tidal stations are in operation globally, in China, the USSR, Canada, and France. A barrage across the Severn Estuary could generate up to 6% of Britain's electricity, but it would have devastating effects on habitats.[8]

Heat pumps □ They produce 3 units of energy for every 1 used to take heat from the ground/water/air by reverse refrigeration.

Combined Heat and Power stations (CHP) □ Britain's power stations waste $\frac{2}{3}$ of energy,[16] as exhaust gases and cooling water. In the US, the heat wasted from big power stations, up to point of use, would more than heat every American house.[17] Elsewhere, this is used to heat offices, homes, etc.

Mini-power stations □ Using car or industrial engines, these can be more than 80% efficient and working within weeks or months.[1]

WHAT SHOULD BE DONE

The developed world must concentrate on efficiency for the next 20 years,[13] with much increased R&D for renewables (in Britain, over £300 million was spent on nuclear power in 1986, compared to a pitiful £14 million on renewables).[1] The developed world must also help the Third World develop clean, efficient economies.

- In the West, improving energy efficiency by at least 3% per year is the quickest, most cost-effective way of reducing carbon dioxide's GE contribution, and solving the acid rain problem.[18] Useful steps include for example: a carbon tax; a tax on oil and its products; a pollution tax on electricity; minimum efficiency standards and energy ratings for appliances, motors, buildings.
- Obtain 10% of energy from ecologically-acceptable renewables by 2000, and 20% by 2025.[14] In Britain, wood-fired small-scale cap plants, fuelled by coppicing existing hedges and woods (and extensive new planting), would give massive amounts of clean power, the renovation of the British countryside, and extra income for farmers.
- For cars: see *The Transport Problem*.

WHAT YOU CAN DO

- Cut your share of energy demand: insulate your home well (in the US, those on low incomes get a grant of $1,600 per house; but in Britain, the loft insulation grant is to be withdrawn, making it hard for the less well-off), buy energy efficient appliances, recycle what you can, use recycled products.
- Only use dishwashers (if you must use them at all) or washing machines when they are full. Dry clothes outside. Avoid fan, convector, infra red and radiant heaters. Switch off unnecessary lights, household appliances, etc. Don't waste hot water.
- Install alternative energy in your home, if possible.
- For cars: see *The Transport Problem*.

15

Overconsumption and Recycling

INTRODUCTION

The developed world is squandering the world's resources at colossal rates, as though they were in infinite supply – and efforts to recycle them are derisory. These resources took millions of years to form, yet we consume them in the blink of an evolutionary eye, without a thought for our children or grandchildren. At present rates, known (and undiscovered) reserves of oil will probably last only another 30 (plus 30) years (see *Energy*); and at least 18 minerals (industry depends on 80) represent a problem.[1]

Every year, industry and business try to improve on outputs and profits, at enormous cost to the environment: clearing more forests, destroying more habitats, gobbling up more virgin land for agriculture, endangering more species, extracting more minerals, using more energy, creating more pollution – in short, fuelling nearly all other environmental problems.

The world now manufactures 7xs more goods than in 1950,[2] with much effort put into persuading people to toss away old possessions and buy new ones – many designed to have a short lifespan. If the Third World is to follow the First World example we need a 5–10xs increase in world manufacturing by the 21st century,[2] which would send the GE haywire!

We must, therefore, realize that indefinite growth in a finite world is the road to ruin.

Therefore, the West – the 20% who consume 80% of resources[3] and energy[1] – must reduce its enormous appetite and recycle all it can.

RECYCLING

Worldwide, about 1 billion tonnes of waste are produced each year,[1] mostly in developed countries. In Britain, over 23 million tonnes of domestic waste are thrown away every year, almost $\frac{1}{2}$ tonne for each person. More than 75% could be recycled, but less than 15% is.[4]

Packaging

Waste has grown enormously in recent years, due to more and more complex (usually unnecessary) packaging, which is designed to be thrown away immediately and makes up around 70% of Britain's domestic waste.[5] This is not hard to understand, when you realize packaging was the 4th largest industry in the US at $29 billion a year even as far back as the early 1970s.[6] The industry is energy-intensive, squanders high-grade materials, spends huge amounts on R&D (adding to the end price), with irresponsible advertising encouraging the throwaway mentality. In the US, in 1986, consumers spent more on food packaging than farmers earned from their crops![7]

Landfill

The average American creates about 1 tonne of garbage each year,[1] 89% disposed of[8] in almost 15,000 landfills and other sites, covering an area of about 200,000 ha.[1] 90% of British waste follows the same path.[9] This is very costly (£720 million pa in Britain), polluting, and uses up a lot of land, often destroying valuable habitats such as estuaries and old quarries. This is an unforgivable waste, with approximately £750 million worth of reclaimable materials discarded in Britain each year.[5] There is no excuse for continuing; nevertheless, Britain, and most other nations, still has no national recycling policy.

Why recycle?

Best not to create waste at all; but once there, it should be recycled, because it: cuts pollution; saves energy; saves resources; saves money; creates employment; cuts the ravages of mineral extraction, environmentally-undesirable paper plantations, and landfill. For example, recycling scrap metal can give a 74% saving in energy, up to 90% saving in virgin materials, an 86% reduction in air pollution, and a 40% reduction in water-use.[10]

Paper

Currently, only 25% of paper is recycled globally;[7] the figure for Mexico is 50%, for Japan 45%, for the Netherlands 43%, for Australia 28%. In Britain, where an average family of 4 threw away 6 trees-worth in 1987, this was 30%.[2] Recycling could save nearly £1 billion in imports, create up to 22,000 jobs,[4] and ease landfill pressure (paper is about 20% of domestic waste volume).[11] Globally, if recycling was doubled, we'd release 80,000 sq kms of forest from production.[1] Furthermore, pulp and paper production are highly polluting and energy intensive, with a paper mill requiring as much water as a city of 50,000.[12]

Glass

In Europe, 30% of glass jars and bottles are recycled.[13] In the US, 100% drinks container recycling would save 500,000 tonnes of glass and almost 50 million barrels of oil a year.

Metals

Globally, 28% of aluminium[1] and 25% of steel is recycled;[7] in the US, over 50% of aluminium cans, 35% of steel.[1] 45% of cans (tin-plated, steel, aluminium) are recycled in Japan, 50% in Australia, 60% in the US, 2% in Britain.[14]

In Britain, nearly 2.5 million tonnes of metal, worth over £1 billion, are buried each year. The nearly 4.5 billion drinks cans we use – which placed end to end would reach the moon[2] – are mostly aluminium, the most energy-intensive packaging.[1]

Plastics

Britain consumes over 2.5 million tonnes of plastic each year,[2] and though the technology exists to recycle most types, pitifully little is. In the US, 20% of PET[8] (a common drinks bottle plastic) is recycled; in Britain, a mere 3%,[4] although the plastics industry is at last planning experimental PET banks.

Textiles

Old clothes can be taken to second-hand shops – in Britain: Oxfam, Sue Ryder, or the Salvation Army. Textiles skips at amenity sites or rag-collectors take them for recycling.

Oil

In Britain, oil from home car services can be recycled at garages or civic amenity sites. Pouring it down the drain is *illegal* and highly polluting; 1 gallon is enough to cover the area of 2 football fields[15] and usually ends up in the sea. (See *Ocean Pollution.*)

Organic waste

Food scraps can be composted into garden fertilizer. And in Shanghai, sewage is recycled and fertilizes an exportable surplus of vegetables. In Calcutta, sewage feeds an aquaculture system, providing 20 tonnes of fresh fish each day.[7]

Others

Batteries contain heavy metals – lead, mercury, cadmium – which pollute the landfill sites where they end up. In Britain, there are no recycling facilities, therefore, you should: 1) save them for when there are; 2) buy those with reduced heavy metal content.

Bric-a-brac and furniture can be taken to charity and second-hand shops.

WHAT HAS BEEN DONE

- In Japan, in the 5 years after the 1973 oil scare, recycling increased from 16% to 48%.[1]
- In the US, recycling is a fast-growing, $20 billion p.a. industry.[8] Legislation requires newspapers to be printed on recycled paper. And some states and many municipal governments have mandatory recycling laws.[7]
- In Holland, it is national policy to divert garbage away from landfill towards recycling.
- By January 1990, all Italian municipal authorities had to make separate collections of glass, metal, and plastic containers.
- Germany, Denmark and Sweden find that separating and recycling rubbish is good economics and ecology. Britain's efforts are some of the least effective in Europe, with only 9% of local authorities having facilities for separate collections.[4]

- In 1985, the EEC recommended a reduction in non-returnable containers. In the US, 9 states have successful deposit legislation.
- In Denmark, since 1981, all beer, soft drinks, and mineral water bottles must be returnable; deposits enable 99% to be refilled.
- In Britain, two new paper-recycling mills were due to open in 1990, with several others planned. And British Alcan plans to build a drinks-can recycling plant at Warrington, Cheshire.
- In Britain, recycled products are increasingly available in supermarkets and other shops.

WHAT SHOULD BE DONE

The never-ending growth of consumerism cannot continue. We must replace quantity with quality, and minimize waste. This means government action and international co-operation. Priorities should proceed from avoiding non-essential items, to reusing if possible, to recycling, to burning to extract heat, finally to landfill.[7]
- Introduce legislation to outlaw complex packaging and to design it for reuse or recycling.
- Introduce a resource tax on some raw materials to encourage reclamation.
- Introduce mandatory separate domestic rubbish collections for recycling.
- Encourage local authorities to give rebates for every tonne of waste removed from the system for recycling, by businesses and voluntary groups.
- Introduce legislation making all bottles and jars returnable and of a standard shape and size.

Eventually, industry's principal raw material source should be recycling, topping up with new materials where necessary.[7]

WHAT YOU CAN DO

- Avoid waste wherever possible; when you cannot, recycle. Avoid what you don't really need. Buy goods in bulk. If a product is over-packaged, complain – and don't buy it!

Avoid unnecessary bags. Congratulate shops using recycled packaging. Share magazines, donate them to the local hospital when read. Avoid aerosols, plastics, and throwaway cups and plates, napkins and, unless recycled, paper towels and tissues; recycled toilet paper is also now widely available. Install a dual flush toilet to save water. Bags, egg boxes, jars are usually welcomed by wholefood shops. Support companies using returnable bottles, ie Corona and Whites in Britain. Buy milk bottles rather than cartons. Reuse bottles, jars, paper bags, envelopes wherever possible.

- Support local recycling schemes; and pressurize local authorities to increase their efforts. If there is no scheme locally, consider organizing one. (See the Friends of the Earth, *Daily Telegraph* county-by-county *Recycling* guides.)
- Ask for, and buy, recycled products. Increased demand will mean more recycling.
- For more ideas on green housekeeping, in Britain, read John Elkington and Julia Hailes' *The Green Consumer Guide*, Gollancz, 1988, or John Button's *How to be Green*, Century Hutchinson, 1989.

16
Agriculture

INTRODUCTION

The Green Revolution, which started in the 1940s in the West, gave birth to modern high-input, high-output (chemical) agriculture, now practised ubiquitously in the West and more and more in the Third World. This led to record yields in the West in the 1950s and in the Third World in the early 1960s – especially in parts of Latin America and tropical Asia (India doubled its wheat harvest between 1965 and 1972[1]). We now grow enough potentially to feed the world.[2] However, modern agriculture is now beset with problems.

PROBLEMS

The emphasis here is mainly on developed world agriculture, as illustrated by Britain and the US; Third World problems are rather different and were discussed in *Rich World; Poor World*.

Policies

In Britain, since World War Two, with its attendant shortages of food, the main aim of agricultural policy has been increased production and self-sufficiency in food. Consequently, food production is now nothing more than a highly mechanized industry, with arable land a good commodity for investment. In the EEC, despite limited changes, the Common Agricultural Policy (CAP) still supports a high-input, high-output agriculture by a system of grants and subsidies.

Grants

Total developed world agricultural subsidies were £168 billion in 1990;[3] around $50 billion per year in the US;[4] and £16 billion in the EEC.[5] These encourage farmers to produce the infamous surpluses, with the EEC destroying 2.5 million tonnes of fruit

89

and vegetables in 1987 alone, to keep prices up.[6] Meanwhile, Third World subsistence farmers need only $8 billion to lift them out of self-reinforcing poverty.[2] (See *Rich World; Poor World.*)

Broadening the income gap

In Britain, the largest, most intensive farms (about 11% of the total number) produce over 50% of output, therefore most of the surpluses. Thus, most subsidies go to those who need them least, with many small farmers, the majority, facing ruin as a result.[7]

Pollution

High-yield varieties need enormous amounts of fertilizers and pesticides, which cause the wholesale pollution of continents, and contaminate food and drinking water. British government policies have to date positively encouraged their overuse, with £1 billion spent on them (plus lime) in 1982.[8] There are, however, signs that we may be on the brink of a lower-input agriculture. (See *Inland Pollution.*)

Food

Apart from the risks of nitrate and pesticide residues, the West's low-fibre, high-fat, over-processed diet increases risks of obesity, heart disease, stroke, and some forms of cancer. More than 75% of US food is processed in some way.[2] In Britain, an estimated 3,850 additives are used in food, with the average person eating 2.5 kg of them in 1984;[9] not all have been properly tested, and the long-term effects of many are unknown. And the hormones and antibiotics, used in livestock farming, leave residues in meat. Thus, it is not hard to conclude that increasing cancer levels are linked with the poisons that pervade our food and our environment.

And now, after its unbanning in June 1989, Britons are threatened with food irradiation, which suits the food industry nicely, as it makes food look good and last longer. It is permitted in 30 countries, but 85% of Britons are against it, and Tesco's and Marks and Spencer (M&S) say they won't stock foods that have been irradiated.[10] The British Medical

Association (BMA) and the Consumers' Association are worried about the poorly understood chemical changes that will occur and long-term health risks. The BMA's Dr John Dawson said it might be used to camouflage substandard food.

Soil erosion

Soil erosion is a major price we pay globally for working the land too hard, with 20,000 sq kms of arable land lost to modern agriculture each year. The US alone has lost at least $\frac{1}{3}$ of its topsoils.[2] And in Britain, hedgerow loss contributes to serious erosion, now affecting 20% of farmland.[7]

Irrigation

Irrigation is the cornerstone of global food production, using 70% of water worldwide, with many countries relying on it for more than $\frac{1}{2}$ their food production. However, it is less than 40% efficient, and its environmental costs include: salinization, declining and contaminated aquifers, shrinking lakes and inland seas, and the destruction of aquatic habitats. One fifth of US irrigated land is being watered only by dropping water tables from 15 to 152 cm per year! In areas of India's Tamil Nadu state, heavy pumping has dropped water levels up to 25–30 m in a decade![1]

Habitat and wildlife loss

Agriculture, with its monocultures of plants that support little wildlife, has eradicated plant communities and habitats all over the world. And each year, more land and more habitats come under the plough. In Britain, the colossal loss of habitat has been mainly at the hands of farmers (development and forestry to a lesser extent), although largely encouraged by generous government grants. So much wildlife is threatened that in Britain over 80 bird species, 60 plants, and 40 animals are protected by conservation laws.[8] (See *Habitat Loss*.)

Factory farming

In Britain, 95% of chickens are incarcerated in battery cages in horrendous conditions; 95% of breeding sows are permanently penned,[7] 60% unable to take more than one step forward or backwards.[11] (See *Animal Abuse*.)

Loss of agricultural land

Globally, about 110,000 sq km of arable land are lost to erosion, desertification, toxification, and conversion to non-agricultural uses each year. At present rates, a massive 18% will be lost between 1975 and 2000.[2] In the US and Canada combined, 4,800 sq km of prime farmland are covered with buildings, roads, reservoirs each year.[12] This bodes ill for feeding exploding populations. (See *Rich World; Poor World; Soil Erosion; Desertification*.)

Slowing yield increases

As the biological potential of the high-yielding strains is reached, yields are unlikely to rise much more.

Monocultures and pest resistance

Modern agriculture is typified by large areas of the same crop, often the same variety, which are vulnerable to pests and diseases. These latter are quick to develop resistance to new sprays and resistant strains.

Loss of crop genetic variety

(See *chapter of same name*.)

Waste

In Britain, nearly 50% of straw is burned, a by-product potentially worth up to £500 million.[8] It could be used as fuel, used in the chemical industry, used to make paper and board, or incorporated into the soil to improve structure. Another example of a useful resource turned into a pollutant.

Energy consumption

Oil-based pesticides and fertilizers (the backbone of conventional agriculture) are an enormous drain on limited oil supplies.

4% of UK fuel is used on the farm. Transport, processing, and packaging of food use another 12%.[8] In the US, processing costs $10 billion per year, and uses almost as much energy as growing the crop. If every nation followed suit, world oil reserves would be emptied in 12 years.[2]

Larger farms

In Britain, Ministry of Agriculture (MAFF) policies favour large, capital-intensive farms at the expense of the vast majority who are small or tenant farmers. Consequently, we lose 5,500 farms each year,[7] whilst those over 200 ha increase 10% per decade.[8] Unless born into a farm, it is almost impossible to become a farmer.

Similarly in the US: since 1960, farmer numbers have halved as farms get bigger. Those left are deeply in debt – on average by nearly $70,000 – due to escalating costs: hence the apparent indifference to the environment.[2]

Smaller workforce

In Britain, 4,000 full-time farm workers leave the land each year.[7] Since 1945, the number has plummeted from over 1 million to $\frac{1}{3}$ million or 2.8% of the civilian workforce, compared to 8% in France and 19% in Ireland.[8]

De-ruralization

This saps rural communities of jobs and incomes, which leads to shops and local services closing down, villages dying. This is a serious problem right across Europe.

SOLUTIONS

Modern agriculture is running out of steam; it is also unsustainable, based as it is on limited oil reserves. We need a new world agriculture that maintains high yields without destroying the soil, the environment, and human health.

- Short-term, Integrated Pest Management (IPM), which uses 30–90% fewer pesticides, is a big step towards a less chemical-intensive agriculture. It is based on biological controls (eg. introducing natural pest predators and weed diseases), cultural practices (eg. underplanting crops with weed suppressing legumes), genetic manipulations (eg. pest-resistant crop varieties), and careful use of chemicals. In 1984, it was underway on about 8% of US cropland, costing $48 million between 1973 and 1983, but leading to increased profits for farmers of $579 million.[13] (See *Inland Pollution*.)

93

- Longer-term, organic agriculture, which uses no pesticides or artificial fertilizers, and is therefore sustainable, is the only answer. At present, though, in Britain, only a pitiful 0.05% of farmland is organic[14] and only 1% of food consumed.[15] Contrary to popular belief, organic cereal yields are only 10–20% less than conventional ones; which is excellent considering the lion's share of R&D and technology has gone to high-input agriculture. In the US, the National Academy of Sciences surveyed 14 'alternative' farms, including an Ohio farm that had not used chemicals in 15 years and managed corn yields 32% higher and soya bean yields 40% higher than the local average. The report concluded that using fewer chemicals 'lessens agriculture's potential for adverse environmental and health effects without necessarily decreasing – and in some cases increasing – per acre crop yields and the productivity of livestock management systems.'[16]

WHAT HAS BEEN DONE

- China probably has the best record for using IPM, but it has also been successfully used in the US, Indonesia, and Brazil. (See *Inland Pollution*.)
- Denmark is subsidizing the change-over period to organic agriculture, resulting in 175 organic dairy farms, compared to 14 in Britain. And in France, farmers in special areas will be given assistance to go organic.[17]
- EEC and UK agricultural policies are slowly becoming more environmental, although an estimated 90% of agricultural spending in the UK is still potentially damaging.[5] In response to the reorientation of CAP, to revitalize declining rural areas, the EEC First Action Programme, 1989–92, will encourage tree-planting on farmland, environmental protection, and recreation.
- West Germany and other European countries have banned certain herbicides in water catchment areas and nature reserves. West Germany is offering compensation for reducing pesticide use.
- In Britain, however, MAFF is timewarped in the past

with only a piecemeal approach for the future. 'Setaside' (scheme whereby EEC farmers are paid not to farm the land) has no conservation value, and ESAs (Environmentally Sensitive Areas) are not much better; both will probably lead to islands of habitat surrounded by ever more intensively farmed prairies. But 12 pilot Nitrate Sensitive Areas (NSAs) are to be compensated for reducing nitrates near water – a step in the right direction, though not comprehensive enough.

- Following public protest, stubble burning will be banned in Britain after the 1992 harvest.
- Organic produce is increasingly available. In Britain, by 1988, Safeway, Asda, Gateway, Sainsbury, Waitrose all stocked organic vegetables and fruit in some of their stores, subject to availability. More recently in some areas, Marks and Spencer and Tesco also have an organic section in their fruit and vegetable departments.

WHAT SHOULD BE DONE

We need long-term policies of lowering inputs, rather than current piecemeal efforts of Setaside, ESAs, and small-scale NSAs.

- Short-term: introduce IPM, together with nitrogen quotas and water protection zones (where nitrates and pesticides are restricted to avoid water pollution). Longer-term: gradually introduce organic agriculture with financial help for the 3-year change-over period (with its depressed yields), price support for organic produce, and greatly increased R&D.
- In Europe, reorientate subsidies away from price support, towards conservation and the support of small or tenant farmers, which will help rejuvenate rural areas.
- Ban aerial spraying.
- Outlaw the inhumane treatment of farm animals.
- In Britain, encourage the renovation of our ravaged countryside with more generous tree planting grants for landowners, discouraging non-native trees and large-scale conifer plantations.

WHAT YOU CAN DO

- Support organic farming, by buying organic food. Ask your greengrocer or supermarket when they will stock it, if they don't already.
- Look for the organic seals of approval. Internationally, 'Demeter' is the Biodynamic Agricultural Association symbol. In Britain, the Soil Association is the flagship of symbols. The Farm Organic labelled products are also 100% organic. The Organic Farmers and Growers have an organic label – and a Conservation Grade label which is not fully organic. UKROFS is the government's organic standard.
- Say no to battery eggs and factory-farmed pig meat; buy free-range eggs and 'good' meat.

17
Desertification

INTRODUCTION

Although many deserts existed 100 million years ago, many were once fertile, with evidence of cities and lush vegetation. The barren Tibet Plateau once sported oak forests; and in Roman times, the shores of the African Mediterranean supplied the Roman empire with wheat. Man has changed this.

Currently, 6% of the earth's ice-free land area is desert, although a shocking 28% more is under moderate to very high risk of being converted,[1] with desertification claiming an area equivalent to 7 Belgiums, or 200,000 sq km globally each year.[2]

Desertification is the tacking-on of an additional strip to the original desert. Land misuse causes the process, but is often worsened by drought. But deserts rarely expand through climatic changes, except over long periods.

WHERE IT IS HAPPENING

In Africa, 22 countries are affected: it is rampant in the West African Sahel, where deforestation rates are 7xs the Third World average. In Mali, the Sahara moved 350 km farther south between 1967 and 1987. Topsoil from Africa, turned to dust, falls on Barbados, with a 3-fold increase between 1967/68 and 1973 – and it is getting worse.[3]

At least 40% of Asia is at high risk, much in the USSR.[1] Inner Mongolia and India are badly affected. Overgrazing threatens most of Australia, puts great pressure on drylands in Central America, and has given the US more severely degraded land than any other country. In South America, exploding populations practising poor agriculture are degrading marginal lands.

CAUSES

Desertification is mainly caused by deforestation, over-cultivation, and overgrazing in dry areas.

Deforestation

The protective forest layer is cleared for fuelwood, fodder, and farmland. This can have drastic effects, as trees catalyse rainfall, maintain soil humidity, and protect the soil from wind and water erosion.

Overcultivation

A downward spiral often follows deforestation. As wood becomes scarce, crop residues and dung are used for fuel (especially in India), depriving the soil of nutrients. Land is overcultivated because of population pressures, never giving marginal soils time to rest. Fertility is drained. Eventually, crops fail.

Overgrazing

In nearly all developing countries, livestock fodder needs are exceeding the sustainable yield of grassland and other sources, and cattle numbers keep growing. In the Indian states of Rajasthan and Karnataka, fodder sources only supply 50–80% of needs.[3]

Animals select the most edible plants, and with the vegetation removed, surface water evaporates more rapidly, the climate becomes drier. Bare soil, compacted by animal hooves, becomes vulnerable to rain and wind erosion. Conditions for plants become more and more harsh. Less desirable plants grow, with grazing pressure increasing on what's left. Finer soil particles wash or blow away, leaving only coarser particles of sand and gravel. Grassland is turned to desert, people move on to other areas and the process is repeated.

Other pressures on the land

In the Sahel in the 1970s at least 100,000 people and millions of animals died.[1] The main cause was not the drought, but two decades of land mismanagement when the region had higher than average rainfall. Cash crop cultivation expanded and the population grew, *pushing* many pastoralists and cultivators towards the fringe of the Sahara. Marginal land was cultivated for the first time in centuries and livestock crowded into tiny areas of pasture, where they shouldn't have been. The land soon became desert.

Salinization

Salinization, or salt build-up in the soil, brought down the Sumerian civilization in southern Iraq around 2000 BC. It is caused by irrigation water lying close to the surface in poorly drained soils in hot climates. As the water evaporates, salts accumulate on the surface, gradually sterilizing the earth. In the 1970s, about 10 million sq km – an area slightly larger than the US – was affected.[2]

Greenhouse Effect

In conjunction with massive deforestation in West Africa, this has resulted in lower rainfall in the Sahel, in many cases decreasing by 20–25% since 1968,[4] thus contributing to the rapid expansion of deserts in recent decades.

EFFECTS

Loss of farmland

By 2000, desertification will have claimed $\frac{1}{3}$ of the world's farmland.

Famine

Arid and semi-arid areas provide 20% of the world's food,[4] but desertification threatens many of these areas. The threat of famine is massive, especially in places like India; already droughts kill hundreds of thousands of cattle, so local governments have set up fodder relief camps! In Ethiopia, desertification was a main cause of the 1985 famine, which claimed more than a million lives.[5]

Populations

Arid and semi-arid areas support 850 million people, of whom 230 million are threatened with desertification.[2] A large proportion are nomads or semi-nomads, depending on their herds for survival. Traditionally, they survived in areas inhospitable to others without damaging the environment. The balance has recently been upset, with expanding populations of peasants forcing them on to less viable land.

Extinctions and habitat loss

Desertification is one of the most serious forms of habitat loss, as it wipes out everything.

Drought

Desertification can prolong drought, as bare land gives off less moisture, so rain clouds do not form. Also, soil dust in the atmosphere makes it difficult for air to rise and form rain.

WHAT HAS BEEN DONE

So far, no one seems really willing to make the effort to cure this problem. There are, however, many successful isolated projects.

- According to *The Encroaching Desert*:

  In Bouza, in Southern Niger, every street is lined with trees, and the town is being encircled by woods. Green belts are being planted around the capital cities of Ouagadougou and Niamey in Burkina Faso and Niger . . . Algeria has planted 267,500 hectares of forests. Ethiopian peasant associations have terraced the heavily eroded land on some 35 watersheds of the central highland plateau, and planted trees for fuelwood and fruit on them. Some 1,500 km of roadside shelter belts are being planted in the State of Rajasthan in India. Sudan is restocking its gum belt, which acts as a barrier to the desert. Peru has begun an $80 million programme to reforest its Andean Sierra. Some 10,000 hectares of sand dunes are being stabilized annually in Rajastan . . . [and] many of the activities of the small, non-governmental organizations (NGOs) have also proved successful, largely because they usually depend critically on the involvement of local people.[6]

- China is planning a 7,000 km forest belt covering a massive 2 million sq km.[2] And India recently planned to plant 5 million ha each year, but is not yet close to this.[3] (See *Habitat Loss*.)
- In the Sahel, between 1975 and 1982, over $160 million was spent on reafforestation projects, but these largely failed because they didn't involve the rural poor they were supposed to help.
- (See also *Soil Erosion*.)

WHAT SHOULD BE DONE

- Apply a more sensitive agriculture at the edge of deserts. Many wild trees and shrubs can help resist desertification, serving as barriers to hold back dunes. Some, such as guayule and jojoba, produce rubber and liquid wax.[1]
- If the Ethiopian government had spent $50 million a year on afforestation and combating soil erosion from the mid-1970s, instead of $275 million a year on war in Eritrea, they could have reversed the advancing desert. In the long run, they have lost massive amounts of land anyway; and emergency relief measures alone cost $500 million.[5] Yet another case of the false economy of war.
- (See also *Soil Erosion*.)

WHAT YOU CAN DO

- Join Green Deserts. (See *Useful Addresses*.)

18
Soil Erosion

INTRODUCTION

Soil is the foundation of civilization, yet its disappearance is hardly mentioned. Each year, 24 billion tons are washed or blown away worldwide,[1] usually ending up in the sea, lost forever. It was estimated that as much topsoil could be lost during the 1980s as in the previous two decades. 2.5 cm of topsoil takes 100–2,500 years to form[2] and a only few months to destroy,[3] yet there is no known way to replace it.

Whole civilizations have disappeared as soil was overused and degraded until it couldn't supply enough food: the great Mayan civilization of Central America went this way in AD 900. Today, however, the problem is more universal: 50% of countries and 50% of arable lands are affected;[2] and in India 39% of land is degraded.[4] Topsoils, typically 15–25 cm deep, are disappearing so quickly that new soils will never replace them on a meaningful time scale.

EROSION HOTSPOTS

Europe is the least affected continent, Asia the worst. And in the Third World, if current fuelwood and land demand continues, much more soil will be degraded.

The worst spot globally is the Himalayan foothills, with about ¼ million tonnes of topsoil washed off the deforested slopes of Nepal and India each year. 1,600 km away, an enormous shallow is building up in the Bay of Bengal, covering over 50,000 sq km, or ⅕ the size of the UK. When this surfaces, it will be claimed by India or Bangladesh![4]

China is losing a massive 5 billion tonnes of topsoil each year, equivalent to 1 cm from all its arable land. The Yangtse River silt load is equivalent to the Nile, Mississippi, and Amazon together. Ditto the Yellow River, which is rising 10 cm per year and stands 7 m above most of the east China plain.[5]

In the US, since farming began, 1/3 of all topsoil has been lost,[3] with cropland almost 2xs the size of California now unproductive, perhaps ruined.[2] Erosion is gradually slowing, but is still 1.6 billion tonnes per year.[5] In the early 1980s, for every ton of grain produced, 6 tons of topsoil were lost! Control cost over $1 billion per year.[4]

Mexico, N.E. Brazil, North Africa, the Sahel, Ethiopia, Botswana/Namibia, the Middle East, Baluchistan, Rajasthan, Central Asia, Mongolia, Yangste, and Australia are all seriously affected. In Britain, in 1988, 44% of arable land was at risk due to intensive farming.[6]

CAUSES

Soil erosion and desertification are closely linked in their causes. (See *Desertification*.)

Deforestation

Shelter-belts and hedgerows soften the wind's erosive powers. Forest protects from rain, especially delicate tropical soils. Over hundreds of years, some of the world's biggest forests were felled in central China for agricultural land, producing some of the most irreparable erosion anywhere. And all over the tropics, where massive deforestation is the norm, massive erosion follows, often resulting in barren land.

Over-cultivation

During the 1930s, American farmers exploited the great plains of the south with new intensive methods of cultivation. As a result, about 335 million tonnes of fertile topsoil blew off the over-cultivated, bone dry plains, forming a dust cloud that partially eclipsed the sun over large areas of the US. The resulting Dust Bowl has taken 50 years to reclaim.

Over-grazing

As much as 400 million tonnes of soil are blown off over-grazed lands in Africa each year, creating haze clouds visible from satellites.[3] In the US, 58% of the Bureau of Land Management's

(BLM) 66 million ha of grazing land was recently only in fair to poor condition, due to over-grazing.[1]

Inadequate terracing

If the steep slopes cultivated in the Himalayan Foothills were terraced, much erosion could be prevented.

EFFECTS

Deforestation causes soil erosion, and the silt or sediment from this is carried by rivers, settling wherever waterflow slows.

Flooding

River sedimentation aggravates flooding, with the heavily populated Ganges and Brahmaputra plains in Bangladesh being particularly affected. The 1974 floods severely reduced the rice harvest, with the ensuing famine claiming $\frac{1}{3}$ million.[7] The 1988 flood (the worst on record) inundated over $\frac{2}{3}$ of the country for several days,[1] causing massive damage. Floods in Bangladesh, Pakistan, and India are increasing in frequency and severity; and in India, the area of annual flooding has tripled since 1960,[1] to 590,000 sq km – an area larger than France.[4]

Siltation

Silt has prematurely clogged hydroelectric reservoirs, irrigation canals, and coastal harbours all over the world. Revenue losses from the 23 year old Cachi hydroelectric dam in Costa Rica are now between $133 and 274 million.[4]

Coral reefs

When silt is deposited on coral reefs, it blocks out the light, eventually suffocating them.

Loss of agricultural land

Globally, 110,000 sq km of arable land (or an area a little smaller than England) are lost each year, 18% from soil erosion,[2] something we can little afford with the world

population set to increase by 96 million a year in the 1990s.[1]
(See *Agriculture*.)

Loss of agricultural productivity

The loss of 2.5 cm of topsoil leads to a 6% decrease in corn and wheat yields. Globally, this works out at 9 million tons – about 0.6% of world harvests.[1] If US erosion continues unchecked for another 50 years, the grain harvest will be cut by 50–75 million tonnes, about 50% of 1980's exports, affecting millions around the world who depend on them.[2]

Desertification

Soil erosion is one of the steps in the process of desertification.

WHAT HAS BEEN DONE

Only the US has succeeded in slowing erosion – by 25% since 1985.[1] And Kenya is the only Third World country with a successful soil erosion programme. But there are one or two encouraging projects elsewhere:

- In Nepal, local people are involved in, and given incentives for, tree planting projects. In Colombia, reforestation and soil conservation of upland watersheds is paid for by a tax on hydropower. In Indonesia, nitrogen-fixing trees planted along the contours of steep hills hold the soil.
- The Majjia Valley in Niger, by the mid-1970s, was denuded of trees, with annual soil losses of 20 tons per ha. In 1974, the villagers set up a nursery of the deep-rooted Asian tree neem, which produced fuel, timber, lamp oil, and a natural crop-insecticide. The trees occupied up to 15% of cropland, but yields increased 20%, so that by 1985, 330 km of windbreak had been planted. The project was successful because the technology was simple and appropriate, costs were small, and benefits were rapid and obvious.
- The famous Indian Chipko Movement began in 1973 in a village near the Tibetan border, when the government sold the local forest to loggers. The forest supplied firewood, fodder, food, medicines and, most importantly, prevented soil erosion, which had already washed away whole villages.

When the loggers arrived, the local women came out and hugged the trees, thus saving the forest. This spread into a national campaign, which saved countless forests and initiated local planting schemes. Women are the movement's backbone.

- The no-tillage revolution (farming without cultivating) has been used on 30 million ha in the US, and in many other countries, to cut erosion – unfortunately it depends on heavy pesticide usage.[3]
- In Southern India, vetiver grass has been successfully used to make thick hedges, which retain soil when planted along the contours of slopes.
- In the US, between 1985 and 1990, about 13 million ha of cropland were planted to grass and trees to curb erosion (and surpluses). (See *Habitat Loss*.)

WHAT SHOULD BE DONE

Protecting the world's cropland will cost about $24 billion per year – a good deal less than the annual $40 billion subsidies paid to US farmers. With exploding populations, this is a payment we must make.

- Plant at least 1 million sq km – the size of Egypt – with trees worldwide to restore and maintain soil productivity and watersheds.
- Establish shelter-belts around cropland in semi-arid areas to reduce wind erosion, enhance soil moisture, and boost crop yields (from 3 to 35%).[4]
- Terrace hilly areas. On less steep land, plough along the contours to prevent erosion. Plant resilient grass on bare slopes.
- Introduce livestock breeds that can survive drought and need little forage, putting fewer demands on marginal lands.
- But most importantly, introduce land reform so farmers do not drift on to fragile marginal lands in the first place.

19

Loss of Crop Genetic Variety

INTRODUCTION

Agriculture, the basis of civilization, depends on genetic variety as a source of new material for new crop varieties, which must be continually developed to keep pace with pests and diseases overcoming crop resistance. But genetic variety is under serious threat – constituting one of the more obscure and serious environmental problems.

CAUSES

Chemical companies and high-yield agriculture

Since 1970, a few giant chemical corporations have taken over more than 400 small seed firms that used to produce a vast variety of seeds for different conditions.[1] With a monopoly on seeds, they can breed crops dependent on large inputs of fertilizers and pesticides (which they also manufacture), regardless of more desirable trends towards low input agriculture and a healthy environment. The very source of food has been reduced to figures on the profit and loss account. (See *Agriculture*.)

The vast range of local crop varieties has been replaced with a few high-yield varieties (HYVs). In the US, around 70% of the area of important crops grows only a few inbred varieties.[2] In the Third World, a few 'miracle' varieties have replaced numerous traditional strains. Before the Green Revolution, 2,000 varieties of rice were grown worldwide, now only 25.[3] Since they are not being grown, many unique strains are becoming extinct. And although not all of these were the best, they may have had qualities needed for future cross-breeding.

Other pressures

A combination of exploding populations, urbanization,

spreading cultivation, and habitat loss are continually destroying valuable populations of wild and semi-wild ancestors of crops. This has happened in the famines in Nigeria, Ethiopia, and the Sahel, which forced humans and their stock to eat virtually every edible plant; with the building of Lake Nasser in the 1970s; and with the cleaning-up of the ancient Mediterranean ruins (some old crop ancestors existed only in protected historical sites).

Tropical rainforest destruction

Disappearing with the TRFs are the wild relatives of crop species, and the many as yet undiscovered species of potential food and medicines. One isolated ridge top, only 20 sq km in size, in the Andean foothills of western Ecuador, lost up to 90 unique plant species when the last forest was cleared by subsistence farmers.[4]

EFFECTS

Risks of new diseases

Narrowing the crop genetic base and inbreeding are very risky. In 1970, a new strain of fungal blight attacked the US corn crop, 80% of which was especially susceptible; almost 20% of the nation's corn was lost.[2] Without the genetic resources to breed in more resistance, this sort of thing could jeopardize future harvests.

Undermining our food base

Of 80,000 potentially edible plants, about 150 are cultivated large-scale, and less than 20 provide 90% of the world's food. The more we bend and inbreed these, the weaker they become and the more new genes they need from outside. In Europe and the Mediterranean Basin, 118 cattle varieties are threatened; only 30 are safe.[1]

Losing desirable characteristics

The Cornish chicken is an old strain, a fast-growing subspecies of the domestic fowl. It was replaced by new, better egg-laying or better-tasting breeds. But as it faded away, breeders needed some of its genes to boost growth rates. They could have been too late.

Loss of revenue

A Turkish wild wheat, cross-bred with US strains, gave resistance to diseases called 'bunts'. This single improvement was worth about $50 million in the US alone.[2]

Zea diploperennis, a rare perennial maize, discovered in 1978 in Mexico, was down to about 2,000 plants. It opens the potential of perennial maize production, eliminating the need to cultivate and sow each year, with possible billion dollar savings, enormous soil erosion reductions, and resistance to at least 4 out of the 7 major maize diseases.

Loss of genetic variety will leave much less raw material for the biotechnology industry, which could be worth $100 billion per year by the late 1990s.[1]

WHAT HAS BEEN DONE

- Seeds can be saved by refrigeration in so-called gene banks. But there are too few of these and their management is sometimes poor, with 100,000/400,000 seed species in US gene banks in danger of becoming unviable. It would cost a mere $75 to rebreed each species for new seed (a total of $75 million), but the government doesn't seem to care.[5]
- An international network of collections has been established, covering more than 20 of the world's major crops.
- Rare-breeds centres have been set up to prevent further extinctions – Britain has already lost at least 20 breeds of farm animal this century. The public support these ventures by paying an entrance fee.

WHAT SHOULD BE DONE

Habitat protection

The only viable long-term approach to preserve threatened gene pools is by making the relevant habitats into national parks or reserves. Unfortunately, few coincide at present with the most valuable concentrations of genetic resources.

Botanical gardens, zoos, gene banks

A second option is to protect the gene pools off-site. But this is not very practical because of: the sheer size of the task; the inability of some seeds to store well or some species to breed true from seeds; the inability of frozen seeds to keep up with evolution; and that all can be lost through power cuts, negligence or ignorance.

A seed tax

With global seed sales exceeding $10 billion, a tax on corporations selling improved seed could boost on-site conservation of older strains, with revenues subsidizing subsistence farmers to grow at least some traditional varieties.

A price tag on genes

Or these corporations could pay for using new seeds; putting a value on them would give developing countries a reason to save habitats.[1]

WHAT YOU CAN DO

- Support a gene bank.
- Visit rare breeds centres.

20
Animal Abuse

INTRODUCTION

We treat animals appallingly. Here are some of the abuses we commit:

Animal experiments

In Britain, over 3 million animal experiments (that's 3 million animals) occur legally each year. Animals are burned, poisoned, electrocuted, shot, and driven mad to test household detergents, weapons, drugs, industrial chemicals and cosmetics.

Thousands of these animals – especially monkeys – are taken from the wild. The usual way of obtaining a chimp (there were only 25,000 left in the wild in the late 1980s[1]) is to find a mother and child, shoot the mother and take the child. Mortality in transit is high, with an estimated 500 chimps dying to get 125 to the US.[2]

Education

In 1986, over 750,000 animals died in experiments in British universities and polytechnics; plus thousands more in science lessons in schools.[3]

Factory farming

In Britain, 450 million animals are killed for food each year,[6] many after living pitifully squalid lives. 45 million battery hens,[7] supplying 90% of eggs,[8] are stuffed into overcrowded cages, without enough room to flap their wings. 60% of breeding sows are kept in individual pens, with concrete or slatted floors, unable to take more than one step forward or backwards; and in 1987, about 400,000 were permanently chained to the floor.[5] Many veal calves are kept alone in small crates in the dark; this was to have been banned in Britain in

1990, but European exports (where it is still allowed) will still reach our restaurants. With the Mad Cow Disease in Britain, the highly undesirable practice of feeding herbivores with animal matter has come to light. And *foie gras*, a 'delicacy' on our restaurant menus, is produced in France by physically force-feeding geese, until their livers become massively enlarged.

Slaughterhouses

Britain's slaughterhouses are in a disgusting state – 90% fail to come up to EEC standards.[8] The killing techniques are so barbaric that most people would renounce meat-eating for life if they saw them.

The fur trade

Millions of animals are taken in steel-jawed traps each year then killed. Millions more are imprisoned in tiny squalid cages on fur farms. A lot of misery just to serve the whims of the fashion trade.

ANIMAL EXPERIMENTS

In Britain over 21,000 cosmetics and toiletries experiments are conducted each year, and although only 0.5% of the total, that is a lot of unnecessary suffering. Many thousands more take place in Europe and the US (100,000), with most major cosmetics companies involved.[8] Yet, in no country is this a legal requirement.

Routine tests

LD50 (Lethal Dose 50%) □ A group of animals is slowly poisoned until 50% die. They are often forcefed with a stomach tube or made to inhale hairsprays, resulting in bleeding from eyes and mouth, diarrhoea, convulsions, and death. This test is almost valueless.

Draize Eye Test □ Rabbits are put in restraining devices and products dripped into their eyes. Unable to wash the substance away because of poor tear ducts, redness, swelling, discharge, haemorrhaging, and ulceration occur. This is observed for up to a week. 7,100 of these experiments occur each year in Britain.

Skin irritancy tests □ Rabbits, rats, guinea pigs are shaved, scratched, and patched with a product, which may be left up to a fortnight. Results include redness, swelling, and cracking skin.

Arguments against

Cosmetics experiments □ A Consumer Association report found 1 in 11 cosmetics users suffered adverse reactions anyway. And in 1986, *Cosmopolitan* magazine (UK) asked readers' views on animal experiments for cosmetics. 600 answered: 98% were against them and 96% would pay more for tests on computers or volunteers. How can we justify such cruelty, when it is of dubious effectiveness and when society is already inundated with luxury items?

Medical experiments □ Testing drugs on animals may be hindering progress because of the difference between humans and animals and their reactions to drugs. A study of 23 chemicals showed that in only 4 cases did rats and humans break down products in the same way. One pharmaceutical company looked at whether rodent tests could predict known cancer agents: they were successful in less than half the cases – flipping a coin would have been more reliable![9] Failure to give Aids to chimps shows even our closest relatives react differently. Furthermore, morphine calms humans, but excites cats; penicillin is poisonous to guinea pigs. And if all this fails to inspire confidence, remember that Eraldin, Opren,[10] and Thalidomide are animal-tested drugs – withdrawn after serious, sometimes fatal, side effects. The only purpose of animal experiments is to give manufacturers a legal defence against claims for compensation.[11]

WHAT HAS BEEN DONE

Since 1984, things have changed in Britain, with more than 100 companies, including Boots and Tesco, selling Cruelty-Free products.[8] As demand increases, prices will decrease.

- Beauty Without Cruelty, founded 25 years ago, is firmly established. Body Shop, established 12 years ago in a tiny shop in Brighton, is now an international chain with 300 shops.
- In 1988, after embarrassing exposure, Benetton agreed to stop animal testing. In 1989, Revlon and Avon, major cosmetic companies, said they'd follow suit.

BUAV – Britain's main anti-vivisection group – recommend that Cruelty-Free products must comply with the following criteria: 'Neither the ingredients nor the finished product must have been tested on animals within the past 5 years, either by the producer, their supplier, or on behalf of either party.'[12]

WHAT SHOULD BE DONE

Animal experiments

Ban all animal experiments as soon as possible; whilst they continue, use only captive-bred or non-endangered animals. New products can be safely developed without using animals. Most natural ingredients have been tested over hundreds of years and are known to be harmless. New chemicals with mild irritants can be patch tested on human volunteers.[12] Test tube techniques can identify carcinogens. And a chemical's safety can be predicted by scrutinizing its molecular structure. These methods take only days and are cheaper than animal experiments.[9]

Factory farming

Outlaw the inhumane treatment of farm animals and ban battery systems for poultry and livestock.

Zoos

Reduce numbers to the minimum required to conserve endangered species; zoos must be spacious and as near to natural environments as possible.

Circuses

Ban the use of animals in circuses, where they are usually kept in squalid conditions and made to perform humiliating tricks.

WHAT YOU CAN DO

- Buy only Cruelty-Free cosmetics; and encourage friends and relatives to do the same. In Britain, Lis Howlett's *Cruelty-Free Shopper*, Bloomsbury, 1989, lists the companies and products. Companies include: Beauty Without Cruelty, Bodyline Cosmetics, Body Shop International, Cosmetics To Go, Creighton Laboratories, Culpeper, Faith Products, Green Things, Holland and Barrett, Innoxa (England), L'Arome (UK), Martha Hill, Montagne Jeunesse, Natural Beauty Products, Nectar Beauty Shops, Tescos, Weleda (UK), Yardley.
- In Britain, write to the Secretary of State (Home Office, 50 Queen Anne's Gate, London, SW1H 9AT), asking him to revoke all cosmetics experiment licences immediately and never to issue any more. And write to L'Oreal (See *Useful Addresses*), the world's biggest cosmetics company, protesting politely against their animal experiments.
- Join an animal welfare organization. (See *Useful Addresses*.)
- Buy free-range eggs and organically and humanely produced meat. Boycott 'white veal' and *foie gras*.
- Write to your politician, asking for the battery cage and dry sow/tether stall to be phased out.
- Boycott fur coats.
- Boycott circuses with animals, and zoos that don't come up to decent standards.

21

The Arms Race

'Every gun that is made, every warship launched, every rocket fired represents, in the final analysis, a theft from those who hunger and are not fed, who are cold and not clothed.' Ex-US President Eisenhower.

INTRODUCTION

The possibility of nuclear war, or war with weapons of mass destruction, is potentially the gravest threat to the environment. Perhaps more importantly, military spending is one of the biggest drains on resources. And although there are signs of changes for the better, global military spending is still outrageously high – passing the $1,000 billion mark in 1987,[1] more than the total income of the poorest $\frac{1}{2}$ of humanity. Between 1960 and 1986, it rose from an estimated 4.7% of world output to 6%,[2] averaging about 20% of government expenditures.[3] $\frac{3}{4}$ of this spending is in the developed world,[2] more than $\frac{1}{2}$ by the two superpowers, alone.[1]

The Third World, which had over 50 military governments in 1987, also spends large proportions of limited budgets on arms, directly or indirectly encouraged by the superpowers or arms-manufacturing nations. Superpowers avoid open war, but support their allies. Since 1945, 16 million have died, mostly civilians and mostly in the Third World, in 160 wars. Further casualties include millions of injured or maimed and 10 million refugees.[4] Tragically, sustainable development could have removed many pre-war tensions. Meanwhile, tens of millions die from lack of resources to help them through hunger, drought, illness, and poverty in general.

CAUSES

Armed conflict, environmental degradation, injustice, poverty interact in powerful ways.

Environmental stress

Both a cause and effect of conflict. Soil erosion and desertification, for example, plus uncaring politics, drive people into absolute poverty, thereby leading to tension and conflict. Worse, the GE jeopardizes security on a global scale, threatening agricultural systems and possible mass migrations. (See *The Greenhouse Effect*; *Soil Erosion*; *Desertification*.)

Raw materials

Historically, raw materials exploitation has always led to oppression and thus tension, initially, in the European colonies, more recently in Western- and Communist-backed dictatorships, where political repression is the norm. Also, countries have always fought over raw materials, land, and geographical features – these conflicts are likely to increase as resources become scarcer and industry gobbles up increasing amounts of raw materials.

The arms trade

The enormously powerful arms trade is a key obstacle in switching resources from arms to development. Arms play an influential part in national economies and resist redirection towards broader electronics, because they make colossal sums of easy, guaranteed money. China, Argentina, and Peru, however, have recently shown it is possible to make quick and significant changes from military to civil spending.

Western financial institutions and governments

Poverty is a major cause of conflict. Third World debt is a major cause of poverty. And Western financial institutions and governments are largely responsible for the debt, profiting enormously by lending money to huge, usually wholly inappropriate, development projects. Then there's the International Monetary Fund (IMF) which provides short-term loans to defaulting nations, conditional on reductions in food subsidies, health, education, and wages – austerity measures guaranteed to increase conflict. (See *Rich World; Poor World*.)

117

Refugees

Military or environmental refugees move over state boundaries, increasingly putting pressure on recipient nations and increasing interstate tensions.

Technicians

With sophisticated nuclear weapons, we have the dangerous situation in which technicians, not the military, decide upon future military hardware.

EFFECTS

Direct effects

In the last 50 years, the environmental impact of war has increased dramatically, from bombs and fires, to chemical defoliants (as used in Vietnam, destroying huge areas of TRFs), to the possibility of biological warfare. Nuclear weapons testing spread radioactivity all over the globe before atmospheric tests were banned in 1980; with nearly 550 of the 900 nuclear reactors propelling craft at sea, each port of call becomes a potential Chernobyl; with the US navy, alone, having lost at least 48 nuclear warheads and 9 nuclear reactors at sea since 1945.[3]

Indirect effects

Opportunity costs □ But the biggest cost of military spending is that for every dollar it costs, one less is available for food, water, sanitation, health, education, welfare. In that sense, it is the single most important cause of poverty.

Consider: One and a half day's-worth of global military spending is what the UN spent in 1982 on its six largest programmes (development, food, population, children, refugees, the Palestinian question).[4] 1 hour's worth is what the World Health Organization spent over 20 years on its successful campaign to eliminate smallpox. 1/2 day's worth is what an Action Plan for Tropical Forests would cost.[3] The list goes on . . .

Effects on R&D □ Globally, the military gobble up $\frac{1}{4}$–$\frac{1}{3}$ of all

R&D expenditures, capital and investment, and scientists and engineers employed,[43] with the US and USSR giving $\frac{1}{2}$ their R&D budgets to it.[1] Furthermore, nuclear weapons research biases nuclear weapons countries towards nuclear power. (See *Nuclear Power*.)

Effects on industrial economies □ High defence spending hinders economic efficiency. This is unproductive money, with no spin-offs and no inherent economic return. In the US, it is a major cause of inflation and social cutbacks. By contrast, Japan – which spends least (less than 1%) on defence of all developed countries – has the world's highest economic growth rate.[1]

Effects on Third World development □ Arms spending nearly always impedes development, especially in Africa. From 1972 to 1982, arms imports were responsible for an estimated 20% of debt in non-oil producing developing countries.[2] Defence spending creates large demands for imported spares, ammunition, servicing, training, and fuel. Precious foreign currency is needed to pay for this, therefore more peasants are pushed off their land to grow cash crops, more TRFs are destroyed, more wetlands drained. Arms purchased are used in turn to keep the displaced peasants subdued and prevent insurrection!

Arms as a source of conflict □ Massive military spending doesn't further global security – in fact, there are now more wars than ever before. Arms spending creates suspicion and antagonism among nations; sophisticated weapons help convert potential into actual conflict; and in recent years, military force has been threatened or used against non-military challenges.

Increased unemployment □ Unemployment is increased by concentrating investment into capital- rather than labour-intensive industries, in which millions more could be employed. In the US $1 billion spent on military aircraft creates 14,000 jobs; on local transport 21,500, on education 63,000. Thus a $40 billion conversion programme could produce a net increase of more than 650,000 jobs. Similarly in other countries.[5] According to the *Financial Times*, 29 May 1990, 'Cuts in UK defence spending could help reduce unemployment by $\frac{1}{2}$ million and add nearly 2% to the economy's growth over the next decade.'[6]

THE NUCLEAR ARMS RACE

The nuclear bomb is the surest way we've found yet to destroy life on earth. Numbers of nuclear bombs increased globally from 0 to more than 50,000 in 40 years, with the US and USSR owning 95–97%, in rough numerical parity.[3] Although nuclear war seems increasingly unlikely (with increasing detente and the realization that to do so would be suicide), we still possess huge levels of destructive power; and as long as we have these horrendous weapons the threat remains. 24 megatons of them, or the firepower of one Trident submarine, is enough to destroy every major city in the Northern Hemisphere; 300 megatons would destroy all the world's cities; and 15,000 megatons, our current global arsenal, would destroy them 50xs over.[4]

The nuclear deterrent

Nuclear weapons are supposed to prevent war by acting as a deterrent. However, since the first nuclear bomb was dropped on Hiroshima, we've had more wars than ever before. The deterrent 'theoretically' works thus: To deter someone invading, you must be prepared to use your weapons. If you do, however, you not only slaughter millions on the other side, you devastate your own country through Nuclear Winter (see below). Committing mutual suicide doesn't make much sense, so why spend billions on something that cannot be used? Prominent soldiers such as Field-Marshal Lord Carver and the late Lord Mountbatten, have come to see these weapons as militarily useless.[7]

Escalation

Nuclear war could begin in other ways: through nuclear terrorism, equipment malfunctions, or escalation from a regional war. The last is most likely, with more states (India, Pakistan, Iraq, Israel, South Africa) gaining a nuclear strike capability, despite the 1970 Non-Proliferation Treaty which was supposed to stop this.

Nuclear Winter

Even limited nuclear war would virtually destroy all life on earth. Detonating less than 1% of nuclear arsenals would raise so much smoke, dust, and debris into the atmosphere as to virtually eliminate sunlight over northern Eurasia. This is Nuclear Winter: darkness all day, every day, for months, halting photosynthesis, the process that powers the planet. Temperatures would drop as low as minus 20°–40° Celsius, killing off crops, large animals, and humans. The cloud would spread to the tropics, and eventually deep into the southern hemisphere. The ozone layer would be shattered, the TRFs wiped out, habitats obliterated everywhere, species becoming extinct by the millions. By the time it was over, 2 billion would have been killed by the bombs, 2 billion more frozen or starved – civilization literally vaporized.[4]

WHAT HAS BEEN DONE (or SIGNS OF HOPE)

The 1990 International Institute for Strategic Studies (IISS) annual survey stated that the Warsaw Pact is moribund, the East–West confrontation belongs to history, and Nato may have to question whether its continued existence is justified.[8] Such are the improvements of recent years.

Conventional cuts

Soviet military spending was frozen in 1987/88, and is to be cut by 15% in 1990/91. Prime Minister Ryzhkov wanted to cut defence by a further $\frac{1}{3}$–$\frac{1}{2}$.[5] In December 1988, President Gorbachev announced unilateral cuts of 500,000 men, 10,000 tanks, and 800 aircraft (although in 1990 this had not yet been met).[9] The number of tanks west of the Urals will decrease from 50,000 to 38,000, virtually eliminating the surprise attack, so long the concern of Nato.[10]

The US envisages a 25% cut in military budgets and manpower over the next 5 years, in response to all this: meaning a $70 billion fall in the $300 billion budget.[11] Robert McNamara, US Defense Secretary during the 1960s, has argued in a recent book that global security has changed so much that the US could reduce defence spending by $\frac{1}{2}$ in the 1990s.[12]

China has already instigated large-scale military cut-backs ($\frac{1}{6}$ since 1979, dropping it from 13% to 4% of the GNP!) and conversion, with the military given lower priority than agriculture, industry, and science and technology.[5]

Nuclear cuts

Nuclear weapons are classified by range. 'Strategic' weapons (more than 21,000 warheads) have a range of more than 5,500 km and are large weapons forming a major component of the main war plan. 'Intermediate' weapons (about 2,100 warheads) have a range of 500–5,500 km and are sub-divided into short (SRINF) and long (LRINF) range. 'Tactical' weapons comprise artillery shells, short-range missiles, nuclear depth bombs, free-fall bombs, and mines.[3]

SALT (Strategic Arms Limitation Treaty) I (1972) and II (1979) were welcomed enthusiastically, but in reality haven't stopped strategic weapons numbers increasing.

The INF (Intermediate Nuclear Forces) Treaty (December 1987) outlawed all *ground-launched* intermediate missiles (2,100 weapons) by 1991. This is only 4% of the global nuclear arsenal; however, verification procedures were an important step forward.

Since 1986, the US and USSR have said they are ready to reduce strategic arsenals by $\frac{1}{2}$ with a Strategic Arms Reduction Treaty (START): so far nothing has happened. Some argue this is not enough, others that it will not halt a single major weapons system or prevent new weapons being built.[13]

In May 1990, the US announced it would negotiate with the USSR to reduce or eliminate short-range, land-based weapons.[14]

This is all good news, but nuclear disarmament doesn't end here, because *only* land-based weapons are covered, with a strong possibility of the arms race at sea escalating. We must guard against reductions in one area being accompanied by modernization, or an increase in another area, as has always happened before.

WHAT SHOULD BE DONE

- Short-term: rapidly run down nuclear weapons numbers, with measures to stop an arms race in space, a comprehensive nuclear test ban, better adherence to the Non-Proliferation

Treaty, and a comprehensive treaty system that includes non-land-based and tactical weapons. Britain should give up its half-penny's worth of nuclear weapons (and bases) unilaterally, as they are insignificant in global terms and only complicate disarmament. Ultimately, ban all nuclear weapons with a verifiable agreement.

- Governments must introduce legislation (not present in any country yet) to convert the arms industry into a 'peace industry'. In the US, transferring $30 billion annually over 5 years from the military to housing, public transport, education, health, and community services, would increase GNP, employment, and other economic factors.[5]

- Cut right back on the military everywhere. *State of the World 1990* suggests we could instead have a much stronger UN peace-keeping force with the power to defend a member country against an aggressor, allowing national armies to be eliminated.[5] Money saved could at last be used constructively.

- Broaden security assessment to include environmental and other sources of conflict. Security can be increased with small expenditures relative to military spending. Funding for some of the most urgent problems – tropical forests, water, desertification, population – would cost less than 1 month's global military spending.[2]

- Establish an environmental early warning system, to stop damage before it becomes a national threat.[2]

We must turn our backs on conflict and focus on the future. The great global repair allows no room for $1,000 billion military budgets.

WHAT YOU CAN DO

- Join anti-nuclear or peace groups, nationally and locally. Learn the facts. (See *Useful Addresses.*)

- Write letters. Politicians and the press can be influenced by informed correspondents.

- Talk to friends, neighbours, and workmates. Ask your political party, trade union, women's group, to discuss the issue (in Britain, CND can help with speakers).

- Remember we are not alone. All over the world – including the USSR – millions are working for peace. If we each do our bit, we will succeed.

22
The Way Forward

INTRODUCTION

The planet is being destroyed to serve an international order that is unjust and unsustainable. Permanent solutions will not be found until we overhaul our economic system. This, however, will take a huge wave of public opinion to force governments and vested interests to change their ways and help in the rescue operation before it is too late.

A new international co-operation is necessary: we must start to look upon ourselves as citizens of Planet Earth, because it has enough resources for all if fairly shared. Currently, however, there is much Green talk and little Green action in most countries. But time is short, and the next 10 years will probably determine whether life on earth will exist in the 21st century.[1] Continuing a business-as-usual path will bring suffering on a scale never before experienced.

WHERE SHOULD WE BE HEADING?

Sustainable development

Global development must become sustainable – that is, it must meet the needs of the present generation without compromising those of future generations.[2] This means drawing on the earth's ecological interest, not, as we do at present, its capital. It cannot mean a planetary standard of living at Western standards, because there are not the resources available; and if everyone consumed as much fossil fuel as does North America, global carbon dioxide emissions would multiply 6-fold,[3] with unspeakable effects on the GE.

Sustainability is a new, largely untested, theory, but broadly speaking it would have to be ecologically sustainable (most importantly), economically viable, socially just, peaceful in all ways, and use the most appropriate of modern technology. It will mean the wise use of natural resources, equitable development, providing the basic necessities for ALL people, participation by the underprivileged, regional self sufficiency, local control over resources. It must grow from within and not be slapped on from the outside. And it would mean adopting all the measures already mentioned in this book.

HOW SHOULD WE GET THERE?

Governments must make sustainable development central to all planning and activities; internationally, we must narrow the gap between rich and poor countries.

The 1978–80 report of the Independent Commission on International Development, chaired by Willy Brandt, recommended an immediate Emergency Programme: 1) a large transfer of resources to developing countries; 2) an international energy strategy; 3) a global food programme; 4) a start on some major reforms in the international economic system.[4]

Many interrelated issues must be dealt with simultaneously. Stabilizing population without reducing poverty will be difficult. Avoiding mass species extinctions may be impossible as long as Third World debts remain. The resources to save the planet may not be available unless global military spending can be cut.[5]

Governments being forced to accept fundamental reforms are the only hope for the future. Countries such as Canada, Holland, Zimbabwe are reviewing their policies with regard to the Brundtland Report, which recommends sustainable development (albeit with increased industrialization). (See Chapter 1 of report.)

Sources of funds

Globally, an estimated $150 billion per year are needed to start on the path to sustainability,[5] coming mainly from the military (a necessary step, anyway, to reduce international tensions). Further funds could be obtained by taxing usage of the commons (space, the oceans), fossil fuels and minerals, perhaps even international trade.[6]

The military

(See proposal for a much strengthened UN-peace keeping force: *The Arms Race.*)

Third World debt

The enormous Third World debt is a major impediment. *State of the World 1988* suggests setting up a fund, managed by the IMF and World Bank, to rescind enough debt to restore economic progress (Canada has cancelled $581 million of official debt owed by African countries) – funds going to those nations setting out proper sustainable development strategies.[5] (See *Rich World; Poor World.*)

Legal means

According to the Brundtland Commission, it is time to draw up a Universal Declaration on Environmental Protection and Sustainable Development, similar to the Universal Declaration of Human Rights.[7]

International institutions

The World Bank, Regional Development Banks, the IMF, and bilateral aid agencies must make sustainable development of prime importance. Environmental agencies, NGOs, the scientific community need strengthening everywhere, especially in the Third World. Ditto, international conventions. We also need a Global Risk Assessment Programme to identify critical threats.[2]

National politics

Consider the environment in national and international accounts, together with an annual State of the Environment report.[2] Consider the environment in all economic planning decisions.[8] Develop national foreign policies for the environment – involving major international organizations like the OECD and the UN.[2] GNP is an inherently anti-environmental economic yardstick and must be replaced by one that measures how effectively resources are used.[9]

126

Financial carrots and sticks

Financial incentives and disincentives will often be needed to bring about the necessary changes. For a start, include environmental and social costs in all product prices, making environmentally benevolent products cheaper than others.

Laws and regulations

Laws are the best means to introduce some changes. For instance, the Swiss have banned phosphates in detergents to save their lakes – this is much quicker, simpler, and fairer than relying on Green Consumerism.

Reorienting R&D programmes

Most global R&D goes to the military and big industry; this should be directed towards alternative technology, so we could soon have many available alternatives.

Energy

A sustainable society will be solar-based (solar panels, HEP, biomass, wind, waves); direct conversion being the cornerstone. Northern Europe would probably rely on wind and hydropower; Northern Africa and the Middle East direct sunlight; Japan and the Philippines geothermal energy; and South-East Asia wood, agricultural wastes, sun. Energy production will be decentralized, breaking up current monopolies.[9]

'Lifestylism' and Green Consumerism

Changing one's lifestyle, although admirable and useful in a limited way, will make only a small contribution to the future of the planet. Government action is much more important and effective. 'Lifestylism' and Green Consumerism mustn't be substitutes for fundamental change.

Public interest groups

These have been, are, and will be key catalysts for change.

Vested interests

Industry, banks, unions, the media, individuals, professional associations, and, especially, multinationals are unlikely to 'give in' without a fight. The biggest multinationals have gross annual sales exceeding the GNPs of dozens of countries, often wielding the real power behind politicians.

The media

Their help would speed things up, but since they are usually owned by Big Money or controlled, if indirectly, by governments/ the Establishment, this is not exactly assured.

Power

We need a decentralized, participatory power base to reverse present trends towards over-centralization, the abuse of power, homogeneity and an uncaring society.

Values

Materialism, planned obsolescence, over-large families will not survive the transition. Frugality, respect for nature, appreciating simple things like fresh air, clean water, good food, less of the rat race, more free time and leisure will replace them. Teaching people 'environmental manners' would not be difficult. Children could be educated at school, adults through advertising in the media. Social conditioning already means that urinating in public, for example, is not acceptable, whilst pouring millions of tonnes of raw sewage into the oceans is. It may be absurd, but it works. And if people call that brain-washing, at least we'd be 'brain-washing' people with commonsense for a change, rather than persuading them to kill themselves with cigarettes or fast cars.

Conclusion

Sustainable development doesn't mean, as cynics would like us to believe, living in caves, or sinking into Third World poverty; it means eating less meat, abandoning our addiction to the car, rejecting excessive consumerism etc. If all this still sounds difficult, we must remember that it is infinitely preferable to the consequences of the business-as-usual path.

To be blunt, we have no choice; it is a sustainable society or no society.

Postscript

If this book only persuades people to buy ecological products, to join environmental groups, to make more use of public transport, it won't really have succeeded. What we must do is to eliminate the monster that is devouring our planet: the international economic system. We must replace this with sustainability.

This could be done quickly and easily, if governments put their backing behind it. The answers are there, the money is there (many necessary moves, like building recycled paper mills in Britain, cost peanuts compared to what is spent on nuclear power and the military), the political will is not.

We, the public, must want this, must demand all the changes it takes. We, the public, must do this if we are to survive. We, the public, have only to make the choice. . . . Remember the collapse of the Eastern Bloc – nothing can stop the march of public opinion . . .

Further Reading

General

Norman Myers (ed.) *The Gaia Atlas of Planet Management*. Pan, 1985.

Lester R. Brown et al. *State of the World 1990*. Unwin Hyman/Worldwatch Books, 1990.

André Singer, *Battle for the Planet*. Pan, 1987.

John Button, *How to be Green*. Century Hutchinson, 89.

Jonathon Porritt (ed.) *Friends of the Earth Handbook*. Optima, 1987.

The Ecologist, Worthyvale Manor, Camelford, Cornwall, PL32 9TT, UK. Tel: (0840) 212711.

The New Scientist, Oakfield House, Perrymount Road, Haywards Heath, PH16 3DH. Tel: (0444) 441212.

The Environmental Digest. Same address as *The Ecologist*. (Excellent monthly environmental news roundup.)

Greenhouse Effect

J. Karas and P. Kelly, *The Heat Trap: The Threat Posed by Rising Levels of Greenhouse Gases*. Friends of the Earth, 1988.

Stewart Boyle and John Ardill, *The Greenhouse Effect: A Practical Guide to the World's Changing Climate*. New English Library, 1987.

Fred Pearce, *Turning Up the Heat*. Bodley Head, 1989.

Ozone Depletion

The Aerosol Connection. Friends of the Earth, 1988.

The CFC Story. Greenpeace, 1989.

J. Gribbin, *The Hole in the Sky*. Corgi, 1988.

Tropical Rainforest Destruction

Rainforest Briefing Pack and *The Good Wood Guide*. Friends of the Earth, 1989 and 1990.

Catherine Caulfield, *In the Rainforest*. Heinemann, 1985.

A Report for the Independent Commission on International Humanitarian Issues, *The Vanishing Forest*. Zed Books, 1986.

Philip Hurst, *Rainforest Politics: Ecological Destruction in South-East Asia*. Zed Books, 1990.

Acid Rain

Chris Rose, *Acid Rain: It's happening here*. Greenpeace, 1988.

Fred Pearce, *Acid Rain: What is it, and what is it doing to us?* Penguin, 1987.

Chris Park, *Acid Rain, Rhetoric and Reality*. Methuen, 1987.

Rich World; Poor World

Susan George, *A Fate Worse than Debt*. Penguin, 1988.

Harold Lever and Christopher Huhne, *Debt and Danger: the World Financial Crisis*. Penguin, 1987.

Teresa Hayter and Catharine Watson, *Aid: Rhetoric and Reality*. Pluto Press, 1985.

Paul Harrison, *Inside the Third World*. Penguin, 1982; and *The Greening of Africa*. Paladin, 1987.

The New Internationalist, 42 Hythe Bridge Street, Oxford OX1 2EP. (Keeps you up-to-date with Third World issues.)

The Population Bomb

Lester Brown, *Stopping Population Growth*. State of the World/Worldwatch Institute, 1986.

Paul Ehrlich, *The Population Bomb*.

Extinctions

Paul and Anne Ehrlich, *Extinction*. Gollancz, 1981.

Habitat Loss

Marion Shoard, *The Theft of the Countryside*. Maurice Temple Smith, 1980; and *This Land is Our Land*. Paladin, 1987.

Des Wilson (ed.) 'Wildlife: the Battle for the British Countryside', in *The Environmental Crisis*. Heinemann, 1984.

Richard Mabey, *The Common Ground: A place for nature in Britain's future?* Arrow, 1980.

Land and Inland Pollution

Rachel Carson, *Silent Spring*. Penguin, first published 1962.

Nigel Dudley, *This Poisoned Earth*. Piatkus, 1987.

John Elkington, *The Poisoned Womb*. Penguin, 1986.

Goldsmith and Hildyard (eds) *Green Britain or Industrial Wasteland?* Polity Press, 1986.

Brian Price, *C for Chemicals*. Green Print, 1989.

Stephanie Lashford, *The Residue Report*. Thorsons, 1988.

Ocean Pollution

John Elkington, *The Poisoned Womb*. Penguin, 1986.

K. A. Gourlay, *Poisoners of the Seas*. Zed Books, 1989.

Clyde Sanger, *Ordering the Oceans*. Zed Press, 1986.

The Car and Transport

Getting There: A Transport Policy. Friends of the Earth, 1987.

Motorway Madness. Friends of the Earth, 1986.

Richard Ballantine, *Richard's Bicycle Book*. Pan.

Stephen Plowden, *Taming Traffic*. Deutsch, 1980.

Nuclear Power

Walt Patterson, *Nuclear Power*. Penguin, 1976.

Rosalie Bertell, *No Immediate Danger*. Women's Press, 1985.

S. Durie and R. Edwards, *Fuelling the Nuclear Arms Race*. Pluto Press, 1982.

Energy

Michael Flood, *Friends of the Earth: Energy without End*. Friends of the Earth Trust, 1986.

Efficiency of Energy Use. Friends of the Earth, 1989.

Jim Skea, *Electricity for Life*. Friends of the Earth/CPRE, 1988.

Michael Allaby, *Conservation at Home*. Unwin Hyman, 1988.

Overconsumption

John Elkington and Julia Hailes, *The Green Consumer Guide*. Gollancz, 1988; and *The Green Consumer's Supermarket Shopping Guide*. Gollancz, 1989.

Alistair Hay, *Once is Not Enough: A Recycling Policy for Friends of the Earth*. Friends of the Earth, 1989.

Resource. (A FoE quarterly magazine that will keep you up-to-date with recycling issues.)

Material Gains: Reclamation, Recycling and Reuse. FoE/Earth Resources Research.

Materials Recycling: The Virtue of Necessity. (Worldwatch Paper No. 56, available from Conservation Books, 228 London Road, Reading, RG6 1AH.)

Recyling Directories (county by county). Friends of the Earth/*Daily Telegraph*, 1990.

Agriculture

Richard North, *Working The Land*. Temple Smith, 1984.

David Mabey and Allan & Jackie Gear (eds) *The Organic Consumer Guide*. Thorsons, 1990.

M. Hanssen, *E for Additives*. Thorsons, 1984.

Desertification

A Report for the Independent Commission on International Humanitarian Issues, *The Encroaching Desert*. Zed Books, 1986.

Alan Grainger, *Desertification*. Earthscan, 1982.

Animal Abuse

Mark Gold, *Assault and Battery*. Pluto Press, 1983; and *Living Without Cruelty*. Green Print, 1988.

Lis Howlett, *Cruelty-Free Shopper*. Bloomsbury, 1989.

The Arms Race

AMBIO, *Nuclear War, the Aftermath*. Pergamon Press, 1983.

Nuclear Free Seas. Greenpeace, 1987.

Rosalie Bertell, *No Immediate Danger.* Women's Press, 1985.

Jonathan Schell, *The Fate of the Earth.* Picador, 1982; and *The Abolition.* Picador, 1984.

E. P. Thompson and Dan Smith (eds) *Protest and Survive.* Penguin, 1980.

Sanity. (A monthly magazine put out by CND).

The Way Forward

The World Commission on Environment and Development (the Brundtland Commission), *Our Common Future.* OUP, 1987.

David Pearce, Anil Markandya, Deward Barbier, *Blueprint for a Green Economy* (The Pearce Report). Earthscan, 1989.

Sandy Irvine and Alec Ponton, *A Green Manifesto.* Optima, 1988.

Derek Wall, *Getting There: Steps to a Green Society.* Green Print, 1990.

Charlene Spretnak and Fritjof Capra, *Green Politics: The Global Promise.* Paladin, 1985.

Fritz Schumacher, *Small is Beautiful: Economics as if People Mattered.* Abacus, 1974.

Erich Fromm, *To Have or to Be?* Abacus, 1978.

Fritjof Capra, *The Turning Point.* Wildwood House, 1982.

Jonathon Porritt, *Seeing Green.* Blackwell, 1984.

Useful Addresses

General

ARK, 498–500 Harrow Road, London, W9 3QA.

THE CONSUMER'S ASSOCIATION, 14 Buckingham Street, London, WC2.

FRIENDS OF THE EARTH (FoE) UK and International, 26–28 Underwood Street, London, N1 7JQ.

GREENPEACE, Greenpeace House, Canonbury Villas, London N1 2BH. Tel: 071 354 5100.

GREENNET, 26–28 Underwood Street, London, N1 7JQ. Tel: 071 490-1510.

THE GREEN NETWORK, Vera Chaney, 9 Clairmont Road, Colchester, Essex, CO3 5BE. Tel: 0206 46902.

THE GREEN PARTY, 10 Station Parade, Balham High Road, London, SW12 9AZ. Tel: 081 673 0045.

INTERNATIONAL UNION FOR THE CONSERVATION OF NATURE AND NATURAL RESOURCES (IUCN), Avenue du Mont Blanc, 1196 Gland, Switzerland.

WORLD WIDE FUND FOR NATURE (WWF), Panda House, Weyside Park, Godalming, Surrey, GO7 1XR.

WORLD WIDE FUND FOR NATURE (International), Ave du Mont Blanc, CH – 1196 Gland, Switzerland.

HOUSE OF COMMONS ENVIRONMENT COMMITTEE, House of Commons, Westminster, London, SW1.

INTERNATIONAL INSTITUTE FOR ENVIRONMENT AND DEVELOPMENT (IIED), 3 Endsleigh Street, London, WC1H 0DD.

UNITED NATIONS ENVIRONMENTAL PROGRAMME (UNEP), c/o IIED, 3 Endsleigh Street, London, WC1H 0DD.

THE WORLD BANK, 1818 H Street NW, Washington DC, 20433, USA.

WORLD HEALTH ORGANIZATION (WHO), 1211 Geneva 27, Switzerland.

Ozone Depletion

STRATOSPHERIC OZONE REVIEW GROUP (SORG), Department of the Environment, 2 Marsham Street, London, SW1.

Tropical Rainforest Destruction

LIVING EARTH, 10 Upper Grosvenor Street, London, W1X 9PA.

ASSOCIATION OF WOODUSERS AGAINST RAINFOREST EXPLOITATION (AWARE), PO Box 92, London N5 2JJ.

WWF RAIN FOREST APPEAL, Dept 64F, Panda House, Weyside Park, Godalming, Surrey, GU7 1BP.

See also FoE.

Acid Rain

ACID RAIN INFORMATION CENTRE, Department of Environment and Geography, Manchester Polytechnic, John Dalton Extension, Room E310, Chester Street, Manchester.

THE SWEDISH SECRETARIAT ON ACID RAIN, The Environmental Council, 80 York Way, London, N1 9AG.

Rich World; Poor World

OXFAM, 272 Banbury Road, Oxford, OX2 7DZ. Tel: 0865 56777.

TRAIDCRAFT PLC, Kingsway, Gateshead, Tyne and Wear, NE11 0NE.

SURVIVAL INTERNATIONAL, 29 Craven Street, London, WC2N 5NT.

CHRISTIAN AID, PO Box 1, London, SW9 8BH. Tel: 071 733 5500.

Population Bomb

POPULATION CONCERN, 231 Tottenham Court Road, London, W1P 0HY.

Extinctions

THE WHALE AND DOLPHIN CONSERVATION SOCIETY, 20 West Lea Road, Bath, Avon, BA1 3RL.

THE IUCN CONSERVATION MONITORING CENTRE, 219c Huntingdon Road, Cambridge, CB3 0DL.

WWF ELEPHANT APPEAL, Panda House, Weyside Park, Godalming, Surrey, GO7 1XR.

See also GREENPEACE.

Habitat Loss

BRITISH TRUST FOR CONSERVATION VOLUNTEERS (BTCV), 36 St Mary's Street, Wallingford, Oxon, OX10 0EU. Tel: 0491 39766.

COUNCIL FOR THE PROTECTION OF RURAL ENGLAND (CPRE), Warwick House, 25/27 Buckingham Palace Road, London, SW1W 0PP.

COUNTRYSIDE COMMISSION, John Dower House, Crescent Place, Cheltenham, Gloucestershire, GL50 3RA.

MEN OF THE TREES, Turners Hill Road, Crawley Down, Crawley, West Sussex, RH10 4HL.

NATURE CONSERVANCY COUNCIL (NCC), Northminster House, Peterborough, PE1 1UA.

NATIONAL TRUST (NT), 36 Queen Anne's Gate, London, SW1H 9AS. Tel: 071 222 9251.

ROYAL SOCIETY FOR NATURE CONSERVATION (RSNC), The Green, Nettleham, Lincoln, LN2 2NR. Tel: 0522 752326.

ROYAL SOCIETY FOR THE PROTECTION OF BIRDS (RSPB), The Lodge, Sandy, Bedfordshire, SG19 2DL. Tel: 0767 80551.

TREE COUNCIL, 35 Belgrave Square, London SW1X 8QN. Tel: 071 235 8854.

THE WOODLAND TRUST, Autumn Park, Dysart Road, Grantham, Lincolnshire, NG31 6LL.

Inland Pollution

BRITISH AGROCHEMICALS ASSOCIATION, 4 Lincoln Road, Peterborough, Cambs. PE1 2RP.

Ocean Pollution

MARINE CONSERVATION SOCIETY, 4 Gloucester Road, Ross-on-Wye, Herefordshire, HR9 5BU. Tel: 0989 66017.

ADVISORY COMMITTEE ON POLLUTION OF THE SEA, 3 Endsleigh St, London, WC1H 0DD.

See also GREENPEACE.

The Car and Transport

CAMPAIGN FOR LEAD FREE AIR (CLEAR), 3 Endsleigh Street, London, WC1H 0DD.

CYCLISTS' TOURING CLUB, 69 Meadrow, Godalming, Surrey. (Campaigning for the rights of everyday cyclists.)

JOHNSON MATTHEY CATALYTIC SYSTEMS, Orchard Road, Royston, Hertfordshire, SG8 5HE. (Catalytic converter manufacturer.)

NATIONAL SOCIETY FOR CLEAN AIR (NSCA), 136 North Street, Brighton, BN1 1RG. Tel: 0273 26313.

THE PEDESTRIANS ASSOCIATION, 1–5 Wandsworth Road, London SW8.

TRANSPORT 2000, Walkden House, Euston, London, NW1 2GJ.

Nuclear Power

CONSUMERS AGAINST NUCLEAR ENERGY, PO Box 697, London NW1 8YQ.

Energy

ASSOCIATION FOR THE CONSERVATION OF ENERGY, 9 Sherlock Mews, London, W1M 3RH.

CENTRE FOR ALTERNATIVE TECHNOLOGY, Llywyngwern Quarry, Machynlleth, Powys, Wales.

ENERGY EFFICIENCY OFFICE, Room 1312, Thames House South, Millbank, London, SW1P 4QJ. Tel: 071 834 9107.

ENERGY MATTERS, Energy Research Group, Open University, Walton Hall, Milton Keynes, MK7 6AA. Tel: 0908 653335.

INTERMEDIATE TECHNOLOGY DEVELOPMENT GROUP (ITDG), 9 King Street, London, WC2E 8HN.

Overconsumption

ASSOCIATION OF RECYCLED PAPER SUPPLIERS, c/o Paperback Ltd, Bow Triangle Business Centre, Unit 2, Eleanor Street, London, E3 4NP.

BRITISH GLASS MANUFACTURERS CONFEDERATION, Northumberland Road, Sheffield, S10 2UA.

BRITISH PLASTICS FEDERATION, 5 Belgrave Square, London, SW1X 8PH.

BRITISH WASTE PAPER ASSOCIATION, Highgate House, 214 High Street, Guildford, Surrey, GU1 3JB.

THE CANMAKERS' INFORMATION SERVICE, 36 Grosvenor Gardens, London, SW1.

WASTE AND RECYCLING, Aluminium Federation, Broadway House, Calthorpe Road, Five Ways, Birmingham, B15 1TN.

Agriculture

THE BIODYNAMIC ASSOCIATION, Woodman Lane, Clent, Stourbridge, West Midlands, DY9 9PX. Tel: 0562 884933.

BRITISH ORGANIC FARMERS, Leggatts Park, Potters Bar, Hertfordshire.

HENRY DOUBLEDAY RESEARCH ASSOCIATION (HDRA), Ryton-on-Dunsmore, Coventry, Warwickshire.

MINISTRY OF AGRICULTURE FISHERIES AND FOOD (MAFF), Whitehall Place, London, SW1A 2HH.

ORGANIC GROWERS ASSOCIATION, Aeron Park, Llangeitho, Nr Tregaron, Dyfed, Wales.

THE SOIL ASSOCIATION, 86 Colston Street, Bristol, BS1 5BB.

Desertification

GREEN DESERTS LTD, Rougham, Bury St Edmunds, Suffolk, IP30 9LY. Tel: 0359 70265.

Animal Abuse

ANIMAL AID, 7 Castle Street, Tonbridge, Kent, TN9 1BH.

BRITISH UNION FOR THE ABOLITION OF VIVISECTION (BUAV), 16a Crane Grove, London, N7 8LB.

COMPASSION IN WORLD FARMING, 20 Lavant Street, Petersfield, Hampshire, GU32 3EW.

INTERNATIONAL FUND FOR ANIMAL WELFARE (IFAW), Tubwell House, New Road, Crowborough, East Sussex, TN6 2QH.

NATIONAL ANTI-VIVISECTION SOCIETY, 51 Harley Street, London, W1N 1DD.

ROYAL SOCIETY FOR THE PREVENTION OF CRUELTY TO ANIMALS (RSPCA), The Causeway, Horsham, West Sussex, RH12 1HG. Tel: 0403 64181.

ZOO CHECK, Cherry Tree Cottage, Coldharbour, Dorking, Surrey, RH5.

L'OREAL (UK) LTD, Mr Lindsay Owen-Jones, Chairman and Managing Director, 30 Kensington Church Street, London W8 4HA.

The Arms Race

CAMPAIGN FOR NUCLEAR DISARMAMENT (CND), 22–24 Underwood Street, London, N1 7JG.

GREEN CND, 23 Lower Street, Stroud, Glos, GL5 2HT.

For readers outside the UK, the following addresses are a starting point:

US

FRIENDS OF THE EARTH, 530 7th Street SE, Washington DC 20003.

GREENPEACE, 1436 U Street NW, Washington DC 20009.

NATIONAL AUDBON SOCIETY, 801 Pennsylvania Avenue SE, Washington DC 20003.

RAINFOREST ACTION NETWORK, 466 Green Street, Suite 300, San Francisco, CA 94133.

SIERRA CLUB, 330 Pennsylvania Avenue NW, Washington DC 20003.

THE WILDERNESS SOCIETY, 1400 I Street NW, Washington DC 20005.

WORLD RESOURCES INSTITUTE, 1735 New York Avenue NW, Suite 230, Washington DC 20006.

WORLDWATCH INSTITUTE, 1776 Massachusetts Avenue NW, Washington DC 20036.

WORLD WIDE FUND FOR NATURE, 1255 23rd Street NW, Washington DC 20037.

Canada

CANADIAN COALITION ON ACID RAIN, 112 St Clair Avenue West, Toronto, Ontario M4V 2Y3.

FRIENDS OF THE EARTH, 251 Laurier Avenue West, Suite 701, Ottawa, Ontario, K1P 5J6.

GREEN PARTY, 831 Commercial Drive, Vancouver, BC.

GREENPEACE, 427 Bloor St West, Toronto, Ontario M5S 1X7.

OXFAM CANADA, 251 Laurier Ave West, Room 301, Ottawa, Ontario, K1P 5J6.

SIERRA CLUB OF WESTERN CANADA, 314–620 View Street, Victoria, BC.

WORLD WIDE FUND FOR NATURE, 60 St Clair East, Suite 201, Toronto, Ontario, M4T 1N5.

Australia

AUSTRALIAN CONSERVATION FOUNDATION, 672B Glenferrie Rd, Hawthorne, Victoria 3122.

FRIENDS OF THE EARTH, PO Box 530E, Melbourne, Victoria, 3001.

RAINFOREST INFORMATION CENTRE, PO Box 368, NSW, Lismore, 2480.

WILDERNESS SOCIETY, PO Box 188, Civic Square, ACT 2608.

WILDERNESS SOCIETY, 130 Davey Street, Hobart, Tasmania 7000.

WORLD WIDE FUND FOR NATURE, Level 17, St Martins Tower, 31 Market Street, GPO Box 528, Sydney, NSW 2001.

New Zealand
FRIENDS OF THE EARTH, PO Box 39 – 065, Auckland West.
GREENPEACE, Nagel House, 5th Floor, Courthouse Lane, Auckland.
WORLD WIDE FUND FOR NATURE, PO Box 6237, Wellington.

FURTHER SOURCES OF INFORMATION

Television
TV TRUST FOR THE ENVIRONMENT (TVE), 46 Charlotte Street, London W1P 1LX. Tel: 071 637 4602.
TVE USA, c/o 2013 Q Street NW, Washington DC, 2009, USA. Tel: (202) 234 3600.

Established in 1984 by United Central Television and the UN Environmental Programme (UNEP), TVE was designed to be the middleman between broadcasters and environmentalists on the one hand and development organizations on the other, with the main aim of informing and mobilizing public opinion on environmental matters. By 1989, nearly 40 agencies had channelled over $3 million through the Trust, enabling it to mobilize a further $15 million for television programmes and media projects, which have had an impact in nearly 90 countries.

The Moving Pictures service was started in 1987 to provide free, high quality films and videos to TV stations in the developing countries, who would otherwise be unable to afford them. To date, TVE has enabled 54 countries to broadcast over 700 environmental films one or more times, and sent out over 1,000 videos to NGOs.

The quarterly *Moving Pictures Bulletin* reviews the latest films and videos on environment and development issues. This is distributed free to 4,000 TV stations, environmental groups and aid agencies throughout the world. In 1989, TVE launched a video supply service to NGOs in the South.

Also, TVE produces accompanying education material for its major documentaries, and aims to provide more in future. It has provided the operating structure for OUTREACH to supply an expanding network of teachers and schoolchildren in the South with teaching materials.

TVE is also developing a library of films and videos, available now to NGOs (and hopefully in the future to a wider audience).
PANOS INSTITUTE, 9 White Lion Street, London N1 9PD. Tel: 071 278 1111. Fax: 071 278 0345.

The Panos Institute, 31 rue de Reuilly, 75012 Paris, France. Tel: (1) 43 79 29 35.

The Panos Institute, 1717 Massachusetts Avenue NW, Suite 301, Washington DC 20036, USA.

Panos Intézet, Frankel Leó út 102-104.IV.40, 1023 Budapest, Hungary. Tel: (1) 136 3370.

The Panos Institute was founded in 1986 and exists as four separate organizations, in France, Hungary, the UK, and the US. It is an independent information and policy studies institute which works internationally to promote greater awareness of sustainable development. It seeks to be catalytic, working in partnership with other organizations dedicated to 'green' or sustainable, development, especially in the Third World.

The Institute has been publishing titles on development for 3 years. Much of the information is commissioned from Third World writers and researchers. Copies of books are often distributed free to Third World countries. Panos Books publishes dossiers, paperbacks, and technical reports. The books and dossiers cover a broad spectrum of development topics making complex subjects widely accessible. Currently, 2 bi-monthly magazines are published: *Panoscope* – which looks at today's development stories in close-up; and *WorldAIDS*, which reports on AIDS and development.

Panos has a specialist picture library, with 10,000 photographs on development and environment, available to publishers, newspapers, television, etc. And *Down to Earth* is a radio tape and script series on sustainable development, distributed in tape form to Third World radio stations, for direct broadcast, or to be incorporated in locally made programmes; this is also available in the developed world.

Other:

The BBC invariably produce videos after a successful series; and the WWF can often point you in the right direction.

Abbreviations/Acronyms

BLM	Bureau of Land Management (US)
BR	Birth rate
CAP	Common Agriculture Policy (EEC)
CEGB	Central Electricity Generating Board (UK)
CFCs	Chlorofluorocarbons
CITES	Convention on International Trade in Endangered Species
DDT	Dichloro-diphenyl-trichloro-ethane
DR	Death rate
EC	European Commission
EEC	European Economic Community
EPA	Environmental Protection Agency (US)
ESAs	Environmentally Sensitive Areas
FAO	Food and Agriculture Organisation (UN)
FoE	Friends of the Earth (international environmental NGO)
FP	Family Planning
GDP	Gross Domestic Product
GE	Greenhouse Effect
GNP	Gross National Product
ha	Hectare (1 ha = 2.475 acres; 1 acre = 4,840 sq yds)
HEP	Hydro Electric Power; Hydro Power
IFAW	International Fund for Animal Welfare
IISS	International Institute for Strategic Studies
IMF	International Monetary Fund
IPCC	International Panel on Climate Change (UN)
IPM	Integrated Pest Management
IWC	International Whaling Commission
MAFF	Ministry of Agriculture Fisheries and Food (UK)
MRLs	Maximum Residue Levels (UN)
NGO	Non-governmental Organization
NSAs	Nitrate Sensitive Areas
R&D	Research and Development
SPAs	Special Protection Areas
TRF	Tropical Rainforest
UN	United Nations
UNEP	United Nations Environmental Programme
UV-B	Ultra-violet Radiation
WHO	World Health Organisation
WWF	World Wide Fund for Nature Conservation
ZPG	Zero Population Growth

Glossary

Biomass General term for all living matter. Biomass energy is living matter which can be directly used or converted into fuel.

Carcinogen A substance that causes cancer.

Cash crops Crops that generate funds for producer countries through their export value, as opposed to crops that provide staple foods for the local population.

Decommissioning The process by which a nuclear reactor, the life of which is limited to 25–45 years, is disassembled, and the radioactive parts decontaminated or disposed of.

Ecosystem A community of organisms and their environment. It can apply equally to a geographical area of land or ocean or to the entire planet.

First World The developed world: 'The West'; The 'North'; the rich countries.

Fossil fuel Solar energy biologically stored over tens of thousands of years, such as oil, coal, natural gas.

Fuelwood Wood used for direct combustion.

Genetic diversity A measure of natural genetic variation, which can apply either within or between species. It is vital to the functioning of ecosystems and is the basis of biological wealth.

Marginal land Less fertile land that will be brought under cultivation only if economic conditions justify it.

Megawatts One million watts, or MW, a large unit of energy.

Monoculture When a genetic make-up is replicated to provide a uniform crop.

Mutagen A substance that causes mutations.

Pesticides Used here to include all agrochemical sprays: herbicides, insecticides, fungicides, etc.

Renewables/Renewable Energy Sources An energy source whose sustained use will not permanently deplete supplies. Wind, sun, flowing water, plants, and forests are typical examples.

Second World The USSR and Eastern Europe.

Sustainability Meeting the needs of the present generation without compromising those of future generations. (A forest that is harvested, rather than clear-felled without replanting, is sustainable.)

Tetragen A substance that causes foetal mutations.

Third World The developing world. Less developed countries (LDCs) The 'South.' The poor countries.

Notes

Chapter 1

1. *Tropical Forest Conservation and the Timber Trade – a call to action*. FoE pamphlet, 1988.

2. Lester R. Brown et al, *State of the World 1990 – a Worldwatch Institute Report on Progress Toward a Sustainable Society*. Unwin Hyman, 1990.

3. Norman Myers (ed.), *Gaia Atlas of Planet Management*. Pan, 1985.

4. André Singer, *Battle for the Planet*. Pan, 1987.

Chapter 2

1. Steve Elsworth, *A Dictionary of the Environment: a practical guide to today's most important environmental issues*. Paladin, 1990.

2. Lester R. Brown et al, *State of the World 1988 – a Worldwatch Institute Report on Progress Toward a Sustainable Society*. Norton, 1988.

3. Lester R. Brown et al, *State of the World 1990 – a Worldwatch Institute Report on Progress Toward a Sustainable Society*. Unwin Hyman, 1990.

4. *Environmental Digest*, May/June 1990.

5. *The Greenhouse Effect*. FoE chart, September 1988.

6. *Environmental Digest*, October 1989.

7. 'The Big Heat', Panorama, BBC 1, 21 May 1990.

8. *The Guardian*, 22 May 1990.

9. *The Environment: the Government's record. FoE, 1988.*

10. *Environmental Digest*, September 1989.

Chapter 3

1. Elkington and Hailes, *The Green Consumer Guide.* Gollancz. 1988.

2. *The Aerosol Connection*. Friends of the Earth, 1988.

3. Greenpeace Antarctica poster, 1988.

4. *Environmental Digest*, March 1989.

5. *The Daily Mail*, 22 June 1990.

6. 'Mother Nature's Revenge', *Newsweek*, 2 March 1987.

7. *Greenpeace News*, summer 1989.

8. *Environmental Digest*, April 1989.

9. Ibid., June 1989.

10. Lester R. Brown et al, *State of the World 1988 – a Worldwatch Institute Report on Progress Toward a Sustainable Society*. Norton, 1988.

11. *The Daily Mail*, 22 June 1990.

12. One World Talk, Colchester Town Hall, 23 May 1990.

13. Steve Elsworth, *A Dictionary of the Environment: a practical*

guide to today's most important environmental issues. Paladin, 1990.

14. Lester R. Brown et al, *State of the World 1990 – a Worldwatch Institute Report on Progress Toward a Sustainable Society*. Unwin Hyman, 1990.

15. *Environmental Digest*, May/June 1990.

16. FoE Air Campaign, August 1990.

17. *The Guardian Weekly*, 8 July 1990.

Chapter 4

1. Norman Myers (ed.), *Gaia Atlas of Planet Management*. Pan, 1985.

2. *Tropical Forest Conservation and the Timber Trade – a call to action*. FoE pamphlet 1988.

3. Lester R. Brown et al, *State of the World 1990 – a Worldwatch Institute Report on Progress Toward a Sustainable Society*. Unwin Hyman, 1990.

4. *Environmental Digest*, May/June 1990.

5. *Rainforest*. FoE briefing pack, 1989.

6. *Rainforest*. FoE campaign pamphlet, 1988.

7. *Environmental Digest*, June 1989.

8. *Earth Matters*, winter 1988.

9. Elkington and Hailes, *The Green Consumer Guide*. Gollancz, 1988.

10. *Help the World Wildlife Fund*. WWF Tropical Forests and Primates Project, 1982/1983.

11. *Environmental Digest*, August 1989.

12. Lester R. Brown et al, *State of the World 1988 – a Worldwatch Institute Report on Progress Toward a Sustainable Society*. Norton, 1988.

13. 'The World is Dying,' *Sunday Times Magazine*, 26 February 1989.

Chapter 5

1. Lester R. Brown et al, *State of the World 1990 – a Worldwatch Institute Report on Progress Toward a Sustainable Society*. Unwin Hyman, 1990.

2. Chris Rose, *Acid Rain: It's happening here*. Greenpeace, 1988.

3. André Singer, *Battle for the Planet*. Pan, 1987.

4. Jonathon Porrit (ed.), *FoE Handbook*. Optima, 1987.

5. Lester R. Brown et al, *State of the World 1988 – a Worldwatch Institute Report on Progress Toward a Sustainable Society*. Norton, 1988.

6. *Greenpeace News*, winter 1988.

7. *Environmental Digest*, May/June 1990.

8. Angela Smyth and Caroline Wheater, *Here's Health: The Green Guide*. Argus Books, 1990.

9. Fred Pearce, *Acid Rain*. Penguin, 1985.

10. *The Green Gauntlet*. WWF, Greenpeace, FoE, 1988.

Chapter 6

1. Norman Myers (ed.), *Gaia Atlas of Planet Management*. Pan, 1985.

2. *Earth Matters*, spring 1989.

3. One World Talk, Colchester Town Hall, 23 May 1990.

4. Lester R. Brown et al, *State of the World 1990 – a Worldwatch Institute Report on Progress Toward a Sustainable Society*. Unwin Hyman, 1990.

5. 'A Year in the Life of the World,' BBC 1, 30 December 1983.

6. Derek Wall, *Getting There: steps to a green society*. Greenprint, 1990.

7. Jonathon Porritt (ed.), *FoE Handbook*. Optima, 1987.

8. The World Commission on Environment and Development, *Our Common Future*. Oxford University Press, 1987.

9. André Singer, *Battle for the Planet*. Pan, 1987.

10. 'Compassion in World Farming' literature.

11. Lester R. Brown et al, *State of the World 1988 – a Worldwatch Institute Report on Progress Toward a Sustainable Society*. Norton, 1988.

12. *Earth Matters*, spring 1990.

13. *The Green Gauntlet*. WWF, Greenpeace, FoE, 1988.

14. 'Prophets and Loss: responses to global warming,' BBC 2, 22 May 1990.

15. 'Save the Children' membership form.

16. Oxfam literature.

Chapter 7

1. *The Guardian Weekly*, 20 May 1990.

2. Lester R. Brown et al, *State of the World 1990 – a Worldwatch Institute Report on Progress Toward a Sustainable Society*. Unwin Hyman, 1990.

3. Lester R. Brown et al, *State of the World 1988 – a Worldwatch Institute Report on Progress Toward a Sustainable Society*. Norton, 1988.

4. Norman Myers (ed.), *Gaia Atlas of Planet Management*. Pan, 1985.

5. *Scientific American*, September 1989.

6. *Times Atlas of the World*, 1982.

7. André Singer, *Battle for the Planet*. Pan, 1987.

8. Jonathon Porritt (ed.), *FoE Handbook*. Optima, 1987.

9. *Rising Nepal Newspaper*, 9 April 1984.

Chapter 8

1. *Rainforest*. FoE briefing pack, 1989.

2. *WWF News*, April 1989.

3. Elkington and Hailes, *The Green Consumer Guide*. Gollancz, 1988.

4. *Countryside in Crisis*. Friends of the Earth pamphlet, 1988.

5. *Natural World*, winter 1987.

6. *Environmental Digest*, February 1989.

7. Norman Myers (ed.), *Gaia Atlas of Planet Management*. Pan, 1985.

8. Paul Ehrlich, *Extinction*. Gollancz, 1981.

9. *Greenpeace News,* summer 1989.

10. *Earth Matters,* spring 1989.

11. *Environmental Digest*, July 1989.

12. *Today*, 3 July 1990.

13. *The Guardian Weekly*, 22 October 1989.

14. *Environmental Digest*, September 1989.

15. Nick Middleton, *Atlas of Environmental Issues*. Oxford, 1988.

16. *Natural World*, May 1988.

17. Whale and Dolphin Conservation Society membership literature.

18. Lester R. Brown et al, *State of the World 1988 – a Worldwatch Institute Report on Progress Toward a Sustainable Society*. Norton, 1988.

Chapter 9

1. Norman Myers (ed.), *Gaia Atlas of Planet Management*. Pan, 1985.

2. Robert Allen, *How to Save the World*. Kogan Page, 1980.

3. Lester R. Brown et al, *State of the World 1988 – a Worldwatch Institute Report on Progress Toward a Sustainable Society*. Norton, 1988.

4. *Woodland and Habitat Loss*. Woodland Trust membership literature, 1988.

5. RSPB membership form, 1988.

6. *Countryside in Crisis*. Friends of the Earth pamphlet, 1988.

7. *Environmental Digest*, June 1989.

8. *Action for Birds – 100 Years*, RSPB pamphlet, 1989.

9. *Rainforest*. FoE briefing pack, 1989.

10. *Rainforest*. FoE campaign pamphlet, 1988.

11. Paul Ehrlich, *Extinction*. Gollancz, 1981.

12. *Blueprint for a Green Europe – An Environmental Agenda for the 1989 European Elections*. Friends of the Earth, Council for the Protection of Rural England, Green Alliance, World Wide Fund for Nature, with advice from Institute for European Environmental Policy, 1989.

Chapter 10

1. André Singer, *Battle for the Planet*. Pan, 1987.

2. Norman Myers (ed.), *Gaia Atlas of Planet Management*. Pan, 1985.

3. Elkington and Hailes, *The Green Consumer Guide*. Gollancz, 1988.

4. Lester R. Brown et al, *State of the World 1988 – a Worldwatch Institute Report on Progress Toward a Sustainable Society*. Norton, 1988.

5. *Agriculture*. FoE leaflet.

6. *Environmental Digest*, May 1989.

7. Lester R. Brown et al, *State of the World 1990 – a Worldwatch Institute Report on Progress Toward a Sustainable Society*. Unwin Hyman, 1990.

8. Nick Middleton, *Atlas of Environmental Issues*. Oxford, 1988.

9. *The Environment: the Government's record*. FoE, 1988.

10. Stephanie Lashford, *Residue Report*. Thorsons, 1988.

11. *Environmental Digest*, August 1989.

12. Steve Elsworth, *A Dictionary of the Environment: a practical guide to today's most important environmental issues*. Paladin, 1990.

13. *Greenpeace News*, autumn 1988.

14. *Environmental Digest*, February 1989.

15. *Earth Matters*, autumn 1988.

16. *Green Magazine*, October 1989.

17. *Environmental Digest*, May/June 1990.

18. *Motoring and the Environment*. FoE broadsheet.

19. Jonathon Porritt (ed.), *FoE Handbook*. Optima, 1987.

20. ITN News, 28 April 1989.

Chapter 11

1. IFAW letter, October 1988.

2. Nick Middleton, *Atlas of Environmental Issues*. Oxford, 1988.

3. André Singer, *Battle for the Planet*. Pan, 1987.

4. *Greenpeace News*, May 1988.

5. *The Environment: the Government's record*. FoE, 1988.

6. Norman Myers (ed.), *Gaia Atlas of Planet Management. Pan, 1985.*

7. *Greenpeace News*, summer 1989.

8. Greenpeace, July 1989.

9. *Greenpeace News*, February 1988.

10. Steve Elsworth, *A Dictionary of the Environment: a practical guide to today's most important environmental issues*. Paladin, 1990.

11. *What on Earth are We Doing to Our Seas?* Greenpeace chart, July 1989.

12. *Environmental Digest*, October 1989.

13. *Environmental Digest*, January 1990.

14. Elkington and Hailes, *The Green Consumer Guide*. Gollancz, 1988.

15. *Earth Matters*, autumn 1988.

16. *Environmental Digest*, March 1990.

17. *Greenpeace News*, winter 1988.

18. *Environmental Digest*, May 1989.

19. *Save our Seas*. WWF correspondence, 1989.

Chapter 12

1. Elkington and Hailes, *The Green Consumer Guide*. Gollancz, 1988.

2. Lester R. Brown et al, *State of the World 1990 – a Worldwatch Institute Report on Progress Toward a Sustainable Society*. Unwin Hyman, 1990.

3. *Motoring and the Environment*. FoE broadsheet.

4. *Environmental Digest*, September 1989.

5. *Environmental Digest*, May/June 1990.

6. Lester R. Brown et al, *State of the World 1988 – a Worldwatch Institute Report on Progress Toward a Sustainable Society*. Norton, 1988.

7. John Button, *How to be Green*. Century Hutchinson, 1989.

8. Steve Elsworth, *A Dictionary of the Environment: a practical guide to today's most important environmental issues*. Paladin, 1990.

9. *Environmental Digest*, October 1989.

10. Labour's Transport Secretary, Radio 4 News, 9 September 1989.

11. Radio 4 News, 9 October 1989.

12. *Today*, 3 July 1990.

13. *Cities for People*. FoE leaflet.

14. FoE Bike leaflet.

15. *The Environment: the Government's record*. FoE, 1988.

16. *Motoring and the Environment*. FoE broadsheet.

17. Chris Rose, *Acid Rain: It's happening here*. Greenpeace, 1988.

18. *Environmental Digest*, February 1990.

19. *Environmental Digest*, January 1990.

20. *Motoring and the Environment*. FoE broadsheet.

21. *Nuclear Power*. FoE leaflet, 1985.

22. *BBC Wildlife*, October 1989.

23. CLEAR, Aug. 1990.

Chapter 13

1. *Environmental Digest*, July 1989.

2. Steve Elsworth, *A Dictionary of the Environment: a practical guide to today's most important environmental issues*. Paladin, 1990.

3. *Nuclear Power*. FoE leaflet, 1985.

4. *The Environment: the Government's record*. FoE, 1988.

5. Norman Myers (ed.), *Gaia Atlas of Planet Management*. Pan, 1985.

6. CND information.

7. *Hinkley C – No Point*. FoE correspondence, late 1988.

8. *Earth Matters*, autumn 1988.

9. *Peace*. Green Party broadsheet.

10. *What on Earth are We Doing to Our Seas?* Greenpeace chart, July 1989.

11. *Environmental Digest*, March 1989.

12. *Environmental Digest*, January 1990.

13. *Environmental Digest*, March 1990.

14. André Singer, *Battle for the Planet*. Pan, 1987.

15. Elkington and Hailes, *The Green Consumer Guide*. Gollancz, 1988.

16. *Environmental Digest*, November 1989.

17. *The Guardian*, 21 May 1990.

18. *Hinkley Point Special Inquiry: Special Appeal*. FoE correspondence, late 1988.

19. Jonathon Porritt (ed.), *FoE Handbook*. Optima, 1987.

Chapter 14
1. Jonathon Porritt (ed.), *FoE Handbook*. Optima, 1987.
2. *Earth Matters*, autumn 1989.
3. *Environmental Digest*, May 1989.
4. Chris Rose, *Acid Rain: It's happening here*. Greenpeace, 1988.
5. *Nuclear Power*. FoE leaflet, 1985.
6. Steve Elsworth, *A Dictionary of the Environment: a practical guide to today's most important environmental issues*. Paladin, 1990.
7. Norman Myers (ed.), *Gaia Atlas of Planet Management*. Pan, 1985.
8. *Renewable Energy*. FoE leaflet, 1985.
9. André Singer, *Battle for the Planet*. Pan, 1987.
10. Lester R. Brown et al, *State of the World 1990 – a Worldwatch Institute Report on Progress Toward a Sustainable Society*. Unwin Hyman, 1990.
11. 'Prophets and Loss: responses to global warming,' BBC 2, 22 May 1990.
12. *The Environment: the Government's record*. FoE, 1988.
13. Lester R. Brown et al, *State of the World 1988 – a Worldwatch Institute Report on Progress Toward a Sustainable Society*. Norton, 1988.
14. *Blueprint for a Green Europe – An Environmental Agenda for the 1989 European Elections*. Friends of the Earth, Council for the Protection of Rural England, Green Alliance, World Wide Fund for Nature, with advice from Institute for European Environmental Policy, 1989.
15. *Earth Matters*, winter 1988.
16. *Conservation*. FoE leaflet.
17. Charlene Spretnak and Fritjof Capra, *Green Politics*. Paladin, 1985.
18. *The Green Gauntlet*. WWF, Greenpeace, FoE, 1988.

Chapter 15
1. Norman Myers (ed.), *Gaia Atlas of Planet Management*. Pan, 1985.
2. Elkington and Hailes, *The Green Consumer Guide*. Gollancz, 1988.
3. *Earth Matters*, spring 1989.
4. John Button, *How to be Green*. Century Hutchinson, 1989.
5. *Recycling, the Way Forward*. FoE.
6. Dirck Van Sickle, *The Ecological Citizen: Good housekeeping in America*. Harper and Row, 1971.
7. Lester R. Brown et al, *State of the World 1990 – a Worldwatch Institute Report on Progress Toward a Sustainable Society*. Unwin Hyman, 1990.
8. *Scientific American*, September 1989.
9. *The Environment: the Government's record*. FoE, 1988.

10. *Recycling*. FoE leaflet.

11. *Environmental Digest*, May 1989.

12. *Earth Matters*, winter 1988.

13. *Environmental Digest*, August 1989.

14. Angela Smyth and Caroline Wheater, *Here's Health, the Green Guide*. Argus Books, 1990.

15. Jonathon Porritt (ed.), *FoE Handbook*. Optima, 1987.

Chapter 16

1. Lester R. Brown et al, *State of the World 1990 – a Worldwatch Institute Report on Progress Toward a Sustainable Society*. Unwin Hyman, 1990.

2. Norman Myers (ed.), *Gaia Atlas of Planet Management*. Pan, 1985.

3. Farming Today, Radio 4, 12 July 1990.

4. Anthony Rosen, 13 Aug. 1990.

5. *Environmental Digest*, March 1990.

6. Elkington and Hailes, *The Green Consumer Guide*. Gollancz, 1988.

7. *Countryside in Crisis*. Friends of the Earth pamphlet, 1988.

8. *Agriculture*. FoE leaflet.

9. Jonathon Porritt (ed.), *FoE Handbook*. Optima, 1987.

10. *Environmental Digest*, May 1989.

11. 'Compassion in World Farming' literature.

12. Robert Allen, *How to Save the World*. Kogan Page, 1980.

13. Lester R. Brown et al, *State of the World 1988 – a Worldwatch Institute Report on Progress Toward a Sustainable Society*. Norton, 1988.

14. Radio 4 Morning News, 14 November 1990.

15. Jonathon Porritt, 'Your farming environment post 2000,' Savills' Breakfast Seminar, Little Easton, Essex, 22 November 1989.

16. David Mabey and Alan and Jackie Gear (eds), *Thorson's Organic Consumer Guide*. Thorsons, 1990.

17. *Environmental Digest*, May/June 1990.

Chapter 17

1. Norman Myers (ed.), *Gaia Atlas of Planet Management*. Pan, 1985.

2. André Singer, *Battle for the Planet*. Pan, 1987.

3. Lester R. Brown et al, *State of the World 1988 – a Worldwatch Institute Report on Progress Toward a Sustainable Society*. Norton, 1988.

4. *The Guardian Weekly*, 3 June 1990.

5. *Environmental Digest*, October 1989.

6. A Report for the Independent Commission on International Humanitarian Issues, *The Encroaching Desert: the consequences of human failure*. Zed Books, 1986.

Chapter 18

1. Lester R. Brown et al, *State of the World 1990 – a Worldwatch Institute Report on Progress Toward a Sustainable Society.* Unwin Hyman, 1990.

2. Norman Myers (ed.), *Gaia Atlas of Planet Management.* Pan, 1985.

3. André Singer, *Battle for the Planet.* Pan, 1987.

4. Lester R. Brown et al, *State of the World 1988 – a Worldwatch Institute Report on Progress Toward a Sustainable Society.* Norton, 1988.

5. *Environmental Digest*, March 1989.

6. *The Environment: the Government's record.* FoE, 1988.

7. Lester R. Brown, *Building a Sustainable Society.* Norton, 1981.

Chapter 19

1. Norman Myers (ed.), *Gaia Atlas of Planet Management.* Pan, 1985.

2. Paul Ehrlich, *Extinction.* Gollancz, 1981.

3. André Singer, *Battle for the Planet.* Pan, 1987.

4. Lester R. Brown et al, *State of the World 1988 – a Worldwatch Institute Report on Progress Toward a Sustainable Society.* Norton, 1988.

5. Channel Four, 4 April 1989.

Chapter 20

1. *For some it's too late.* WWF leaflet, 1988.

2. Paul Ehrlich, *Extinction.* Gollancz, 1981.

3. National Anti-vivisection Society literature.

4. *Countryside in Crisis.* Friends of the Earth pamphlet, 1988.

5. 'Compassion in World Farming' literature.

6. Jonathon Porritt (ed.), *FoE Handbook.* Optima, 1987.

7. Elkington and Hailes, *The Green Consumer Guide.* Gollancz, 1988.

8. John Button, *How to be Green.* Century Hutchinson, 1989.

9. *Environmental Digest*, July 1989.

10. BUAV leaflet.

11. 11th Hour Group leaflet.

12. Magazine for the 'Choose Cruelty-Free Campaign' organized by BUAV.

Chapter 21

1. André Singer, *Battle for the Planet.* Pan, 1987.

2. The World Commission on Environment and Development, *Our Common Future.* Oxford University Press, 1987.

3. Steve Elsworth, *A Dictionary of the Environment: a practical guide to today's most important environmental issues.* Paladin, 1990.

4. Norman Myers (ed.), *Gaia Atlas of Planet Management.* Pan, 1985.

5. Lester R. Brown et al, *State of the World 1990 – a Worldwatch Institute Report on Progress Toward a Sustainable Society*. Unwin Hyman, 1990.

6. *Sanity*, July/August 1990.

7. CND information.

8. *The Guardian Weekly*, 3 June 1990.

9. *Nature*, 24 May 1990.

10. *The Guardian Weekly*, 15 October 1989.

11. *The Guardian*, 8 May 1990.

12. *Environmental Digest*, October 1989.

13. *The Guardian Weekly*, 10 June 1990.

14. *The Guardian Weekly*, 13 May 1990.

Chapter 22

1. 'World Leaders Bergen Debate,' BBC 1, 22 May 1990.

2. *Our Common Future, A Reader's Guide*. IIED/Earthscan, 1987.

3. One World Talk, Colchester Town Hall, 23 May 1990.

4. Norman Myers (ed.), *Gaia Atlas of Planet Management*. Pan, 1985.

5. Lester R. Brown et al, *State of the World 1988 – a Worldwatch Institute Report on Progress Toward a Sustainable Society*. Norton, 1988.

6. Thijs De La Court, *Beyond Brundtland: green development in the 1990's*. Zed Books, 1990.

7. The World Commission on Environment and Development, *Our Common Future*. Oxford University Press, 1987.

8. David Pearce, Anil Markandya, Edward B. Barbier, *Blueprint for a Green Economy*. Earthscan, 1989.

9. Lester R. Brown et al, *State of the World 1990 – a Worldwatch Institute Report on Progress Toward a Sustainable Society*. Unwin Hyman, 1990.

Index